FUTURE SKILL DEMAND AND SUPPLY

The Policy Studies Institute (PSI) is one of Europe's leading independent research organisations undertaking studies of economic, industrial and social policy, and the workings of political institutions.

PSI is a registered charity, run on a non-profit basis, and is not associated with any political party, pressure group or commercial interest.

PSI attaches great importance to covering a wide range of subject areas with its multi-disciplinary approach. The Institute's researchers are organised in groups which currently cover the following programmes:

Crime, Justice and Youth Studies – Employment and Society – Ethnic Equality and Diversity – European Industrial Development – Family Finances – Information and Citizenship – Information and Cultural Studies – Labour Markets, Employers and the State – Social Care and Health Studies – Work, Benefits and Social Participation

This publication arises from the Labour Markets, Employers and the State group and is one of over 30 publications made available by the Institute each year.

Information about the work of PSI and a catalogue of available books can be obtained from:

External Relations Department, PSI
100 Park Village East, London NW1 3SR

Future Skill Demand and Supply

Edited by Hilary Metcalf

POLICY STUDIES INSTITUTE
London

The publishing imprint of the independent
POLICY STUDIES INSTITUTE
100 Park Village East, London NW1 3SR
Telephone: 0171 468 0468   Fax: 0171 388 0914

© This collection Policy Studies Institute 1995

All rights reserved. No part of this publication may be reproduced, stored in a retrieval system or transmitted, in any form or by any means, electronic or otherwise, without the prior permission of the Policy Studies Institute

ISBN 0 85374 664 8

PSI Research Report 798

A CIP catalogue record of this book is available from the British Library.

1 2 3 4 5 6 7 8 9

PSI publications are available from
BEBC Distribution Ltd
P O Box 1496, Poole, Dorset, BH12 3YD

Books will normally be despatched within 24 hours. Cheques should be made payable to BEBC Distribution Ltd.

Credit card and telephone/fax orders may be placed on the following freephone numbers:

FREEPHONE: 0800 262260
FREEFAX: 0800 262266

Booktrade representation (UK & Eire):
Broadcast Books
24 De Montfort Road, London SW16 1LW
Telephone: 0181 677 5129

PSI subscriptions are available from PSI's subscription agent
Carfax Publishing Company Ltd
P O Box 25, Abingdon, Oxford OX14 3UE

Laserset by Policy Studies Institute
Printed in Great Britain by Latimer Trend and Co Ltd

Contents

1 **Introduction** 1
   Hilary Metcalf, Policy Studies Institute

2 **Skill needs to the end of the century** 6
   Rob Wilson, Institute for Employment Research,
   University of Warwick

3 **Graduates: shortage or glut?** 33
   Helen Connor, Institute for Employment Studies

4 **As the labour market for scientists and technologists
   becomes more international do we need to train more?** 45
   Richard Pearson, Institute for Employment Studies

5 **The future of low-skilled jobs** 56
   Ken Ducatel, PREST, University of Manchester

6 **Can our education and training system deliver?
   Britain's comparative performance** 85
   Peter Robinson, CEPR, London School of Economics

7 **Training policy for competitiveness: time for a new
   perspective** 110
   Ewart Keep, IRRU, Warwick University and *Ken Mayhew,*
   Pembroke College, Oxford

Acknowledgement

The Policy Studies Institute gratefully acknowledges the financial support of the Department for Education and Employment for the *Skills Focus* programme, in which series of conferences these papers were presented.

The views expressed in this report are those of the authors and not necessarily those of the Department for Education and Employment or any other government organisation or department.

1 Introduction

Hilary Metcalf

An increasing body of evidence suggests that investment in education and training is necessary for enhanced economic performance and that skill development is essential to economic advancement in the face of global competition. Although this link is not undisputed, governments worldwide have based their policies on these beliefs. However, agreement on the importance of education and training neither tells us which skills are required nor the policies which will lead to their development.

The shortages and gluts we have been experiencing give seemingly conflicting messages on the nature of skills needed. Much emphasis is placed on the importance of developing an economy based on a highly educated and skilled workforce, capable of responding to rapid changes, but unemployment is high among graduates in general and among scientists and technologists in particular. This may be a cyclical phenomenon, which may disappear with economic recovery. However, it may be a symptom of other difficulties.

A second difficulty arises out of predictions of structural and organisational changes. On the one hand, shifts in the balance of industry to higher-skilled areas, technical change and changes in human resourcing practices all reinforce the need for higher skills. On the other hand, growth in less skilled industries, such as tourism and leisure and personal services, and technical change leading to deskilling continue to be predicted. While these changes are not incompatible (and indeed appear to be occurring in tandem), they leave confusion over the mix of skills required and the direction education and training policies should take.

These are the issues that this volume of papers, first presented at a conference in the *Skills Focus* series sponsored by the Employment Department, aimed to address: the United Kingdom's skill needs to the end of the century and the educational and vocational policies for their delivery.

The problem of skills development in the United Kingdom is commonly seen as one of supply: not enough people are produced with the necessary skills. The solution is then seen in terms of increasing state education and training provision, increasing employer support for training and encouraging individuals to invest in their own skill development. However, the evidence in this volume seems to suggest another problem, that of lack of demand for skills in the economy and the fact that skills are not utilised in appropriate jobs. International comparisons of qualifications are presented which show that the United Kingdom's supply performance is not poor: output of graduates (Connor, Robinson), of scientists and technologists (Pearson) and of the different levels of school qualifications (Robinson) are, in international terms, on a par with other major nations. At the same time, evidence is given of lack of demand for skills. This shows up most dramatically in the unemployment and underemployment of graduates and of graduate scientists and technologists. Ewart Keep and Ken Mayhew in Chapter 6 present a comprehensive analysis of the underlying structural problems which may result in this lack of demand. These findings are crucial to the formulation of policy: if the problem lies in demand rather than supply then increasing the supply of skills will be of little effect. Policy should turn instead to addressing the lack of demand for skills.

The papers

Rob Wilson, in Chapter 2, paints a broad picture of skill needs over the next five years. Cyclical recovery combined with a continuation of the trend in women's participation is expected to lead to growth in the labour force, although this will be somewhat mitigated by a decline in the activity rate of older people (taking early retirement) and younger people (continuing in education). The total labour force is projected to rise to 29 million, with women forming 46 per cent of this. Unemployment is expected to decline, but not dramatically.

The pattern of change in employment which has been seen in the last decade is expected to continue, with a decline in jobs in primary and manufacturing industries offset by an increase in service employment, especially in hotels and catering, other services, health and education. These changes are likely to result in the increased feminisation of employment and an increased incidence of part-time employment. Much of the growth is expected to be in low paid and low status jobs. Self-employment is also expected to continue to grow, mainly in the service sector.

Occupationally, much employment is predicted to continue to follow previous trends. Changes in technology and in the way work is organised are expected to continue to favour well-qualified, highly trained, white-collar, non-manual occupations at the expense of poorly qualified, untrained, blue-collar, manual occupations. Managerial occupations are expected to see by far the largest increase in employment in the next few years, although personal and protective service occupations are also expected to show modest growth. However, clerical and secretarial employment is considered to have peaked and will decline in the next five years.

The following two chapters consider aspects of the future supply and demand for high-level skills. Helen Connor examines the labour market for graduates in Chapter 3 and Richard Pearson the future for scientists and technologists in Chapter 4. Connor discusses the increasing diversity within the higher education system, the broadening of the graduate market and employer concerns about skill deficiencies. She suggests that the current problem of graduate unemployment is largely cyclical, exacerbated by the massive expansion of higher education in the last few years. This expansion has not only increased the supply of graduates, but also resulted in much greater diversity in the range and quality of their skills. Connor reports growing dissatisfaction among employers with the skills of graduates, particularly in business awareness and communication. The consequence of the apparent over-supply has been a growth of graduates in what are considered non-graduate jobs. She suggests that this pattern of underemployment and unemployment is likely to continue. While demand for graduates, per se, is likely to rise, she expects this to be outpaced by increases in graduate output. Consequently, graduates will have to continue to lower their expectations and will continue to expand in 'non-graduate jobs'.

Commentators and politicians frequently emphasise the importance to economic growth of producing more graduate scientists and engineers, lamenting the low number of people studying these subjects. In Chapter 4, Pearson offers a very different perspective. Over the 1980s and 1990s, the output of graduate engineers and scientists has grown massively and he presents evidence to show that Britain is not lagging significantly in its supply of scientists and technologists. At the same time, in Britain, unemployment among this group has been higher than the graduate average. Pearson shows that the number of jobs for research scientists and engineers is low by international standards. He concludes that a major problem in this area is one of demand rather than supply and that an expansion of supply would offer little benefit unless demand were enhanced.

The emphasis on growth areas of the economy and on the importance of high-level skills should not lead to the neglect of other skill needs. First, Wilson, in Chapter 2, points out that growth will not be confined to highly skilled occupations or industries, with personal and protective services and hotel and catering expected to expand. Second, the maintenance of the existing stock of skills is important while, third, training and education for declining occupations is needed. Wilson points out that recruitment difficulties can appear in declining, as well as growing, sectors, with the former exacerbated by new entrants to the labour market preferring to seek jobs in expanding (and therefore, seemingly, more secure) sectors.

Ken Ducatel continues the theme of lower-skilled jobs in Chapter 5. He discusses how changes in management practices, technology and industry will result in the continuance of a significant number of low-skilled jobs. He argues that such jobs are necessary both to the economic well-being of the country and to offer employment opportunities to all. However, he points out that the skill level overall is likely to grow, with a higher basic level of skills required in some of the lower-skilled jobs. In particular, more jobs are expected to require literacy, communication skills, computer skills and the ability to respond to change.

Against this background, the final two chapters look at education and training systems and policies. In Chapter 6, Peter Robinson suggests that the 'skills revolution' sought in the late 1980s has occurred. Difficulties over comparability of international data and the separation in analysis of educational and vocational achievement mean that this success is often overlooked. He argues that the output of our education and training system is broadly in line with other countries with a similar level of GDP. For him, the need to strive for a higher level of attainment is not clear, as he questions the causal link between educational attainment and economic performance.

Ewart Keep and Ken Mayhew return, in Chapter 7, to the issue of demand in their proposals for a national training policy. They consider that Britain has experienced weak demand for skills, which in turn has resulted in supply difficulties. They argue that features of human resourcing, the structure of the economy and capital markets combine to weaken the demand for skills and that there are deep-seated structural factors impeding moves towards a high-skilled, high-productivity, high-wage economy. In the face of this, Keep and Mayhew consider that training policies which concentrate on the supply of skills are inadequate. They conclude that a multi-pronged training strategy is necessary, requiring the coordination of a range of labour market, competitive and product market strategies.

2 Skill needs to the end of the century

Rob Wilson

Abstract
This chapter focuses on longer-term developments in the market for skills, based around the latest projections of the UK labour market produced by the Institute for Employment Research. The underlying macroeconomic and industrial employment scenario is discussed and implications for education and training provision drawn out.

Introduction and summary[1]
The Institute for Employment Research first began producing forward looking assessments of the demand for skills almost 20 years ago. From the beginning it was regarded as essential that such an assessment be grounded in a view about the development of the economy in general. The Institute's projections have therefore been produced using a detailed multisectoral model of the economy, initially designed by Professor Stone and colleagues in Cambridge. More recently the task of maintaining and improving the model has passed to Cambridge Econometrics under the direction of Terry Barker. Throughout this process the Institute has been involved in data processing and model development, with particular emphasis on the labour market.[2]

The main aim of this chapter is to set out the key results of the Institute's latest projections which look forward to the year 2001. Only a few years ago 2001 conjured up images of science fiction rather than impending reality. The position today is that current decisions with regard to education and training policy will have crucial implications for the out-turn only 5 or 6 years hence.

The chapter begins with a brief discussion of the macroeconomic situation facing the UK economy and outlines likely developments in the next few years. The projections were prepared during the summer of 1994 and therefore do not take full account of all the detailed measures announced in the November 1994 budget. Nevertheless it is unlikely that these would significantly alter the main thrust of the results presented here.

Developments in the industrial structure of the economy are a key determinant of the changing pattern of demand for skills. These changes are the product of the confluence of many interacting influences, some of the more important of which are highlighted on pages 12-13. There are few surprises here, the story being one of continuing job losses in primary and manufacturing industries offset by increases in services.

The changing industrial pattern of employment also has important implications for other aspects of employment structure, notably the rising share of female employment, increasing incidence of part-time work and the continuing growth in self-employment. Likely future developments are summarised and discussed.

A key focus of this chapter is occupational employment prospects. Recent trends are reviewed in the light of the latest Census of Population evidence and revised projections reflecting changes in technology and the way in which work is organised have tended to reinforce each other in recent years. In simple terms both factors have favoured well-qualified, highly trained, white-collar, non-manual occupations at the expense of poorly qualified, untrained, blue-collar, manual occupations.

There are, of course, some exceptions to this trend but for the most part, employment structures are likely to continue to move in this direction. Perhaps the most surprising result is that, despite much talk of white-collar recessions and management delayering, the Institute has (if anything) tended to underestimate the growth in employment among managerial occupations. This group is expected to see by far the largest increase in employment opportunities in the next few years. Otherwise, the future trends tend to represent a continuation of those observed in recent years, with the exception of clerical and secretarial occupations, where employment appears to have peaked and is now entering a phase of decline.

The section concludes by drawing out the implications of these results for education and training provision. It is argued that areas of employment growth are not the only places where emphasis needs to be placed. Issues such as maintaining the existing stock of skills are also important. Moreover educational and training policy should not necessarily operate in a purely passive fashion, responding to the perceived requirements of the labour market. There is considerable evidence that active education training measures can influence the growth path of the economy. A case can therefore be made to provide education and training as a means of enhancing competitiveness and raising the rate of economic growth.

Macroeconomic outlook

Despite continuing concerns about the strength of consumer confidence and fears of an acceleration in inflation rates, it seems clear that the UK economy is continuing its sustained recovery from the prolonged recession of the early 1990s. Tight fiscal and monetary policy has meant that the pace of change has remained modest compared to some previous upturns. The government's aim of phasing in tax increases in order to avoid over-rapid expansion, while not nipping in the bud a sometimes hesitant recovery, appears to be paying off. However, some concerns about both failing domestic demand and inflation remain.

The international economic environment is reasonably optimistic, with recovery from recession in many other developed economies well under way. This suggests that the outlook for UK exporters is likely to remain good for some time to come although it also raises concerns about possible overheating of the world economy over the medium term.

The growth of GDP in 1994 is now estimated to be just under 4 per cent, with some slowing in 1995 as the tax increases first announced in the November 1993 budget take effect. Over the medium term the economy is projected to settle down to a rate of growth of around 2.5 per cent per annum (see Figure 2.1).

The recovery has been sustained by modest increases in consumer expenditure which, although not rising especially rapidly compared to previous boom periods, has nevertheless shown sustained growth, having risen every quarter since the beginning of 1992. As the effects of deferred spending wear off and as the impact of tax increases bite, this is expected to slow down in 1995. The baton is expected to be taken up by gross fixed capital formation

Skill needs to the end of the century

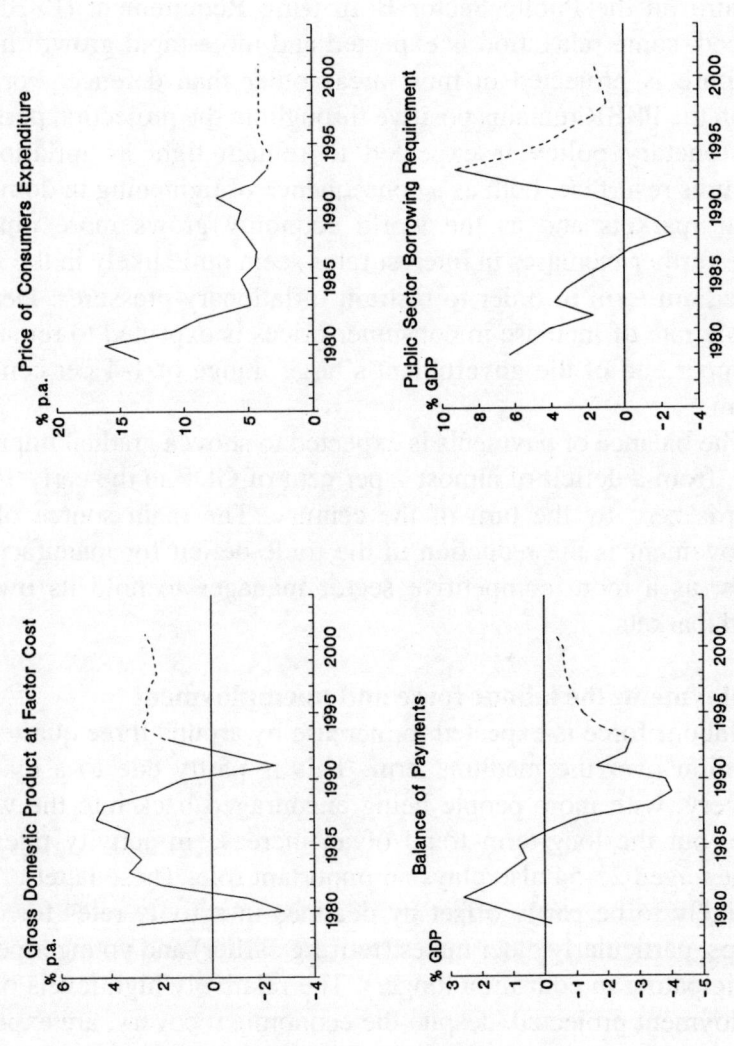

Figure 2.1 UK macroeconomic prospects

Source: IER Estimates

Future skill demand and supply

and by export demand, resulting in a fairly balanced pattern of growth in the mid-1990s.

Government expenditure has been sharply curtailed in recent years and this pattern is expected to continue in the immediate future. However, as unemployment falls, tax revenues rise and pressure on the Public Sector Borrowing Requirement (PSBR) is reduced, some relaxation is expected and more rapid growth in expenditure is projected in most areas other than defence. For this reason the PSBR remains positive throughout the projection period.

Monetary policy is expected to remain tight as inflationary pressures resurface, both as a consequence of tightening in domestic labour markets and as the world economy grows more rapidly. Some further increases in interest rates seem quite likely in the short to medium term in order to restrain inflationary pressures. Despite this the rate of increase in consumer prices is expected to remain at the upper end of the government's target range of 1-4 per cent per annum.

The balance of payments is expected to show a gradual improvement, from a deficit of almost 2 per cent of GDP in the early 1990s towards zero by the turn of the century. The main source of the improvement is the reduction in the trade deficit for manufactured goods, as a more competitive sector manages to hold its own in world markets.

Employment, the labour force and unemployment
The labour force is expected to increase by around three quarters of a million over the medium term. This is partly due to a cyclical recovery, with more people being encouraged back into the workforce, but the long-term trend of an increase in activity rates for women aged 25-54 also plays an important role. These latter effects are likely to be partly offset by declines in activity rates for other groups, particularly older males (retiring earlier) and younger people (participating in education longer). The relatively high levels of unemployment projected, despite the economic recovery, are expected to discourage many people from actively seeking work, and to accelerate trends to early retirement.

The population projections are based on the 1992-based projections from the Government Actuary's Department (GAD) and the Office of Population Censuses and Surveys (OPCS). These use data

Skill needs to the end of the century

Figure 2.2 The labour force, employment and unemployment

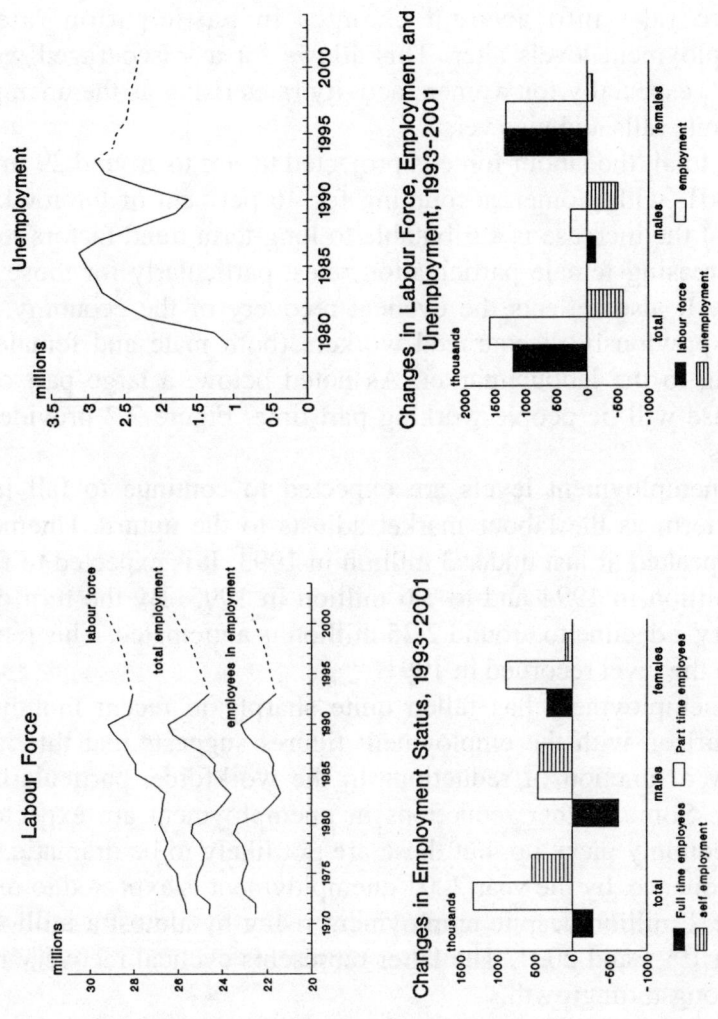

Source: IER Estimates

from the 1991 Census of Population, updated using information on fertility, mortality and migration. There are slightly upward revisions compared with previous estimates.

The labour force projections are based on official forecasts of activity rates by the former Employment Department (1994) modified to take into account changes in participation rates as unemployment levels alter. This allows for a 'discouraged worker effect', especially for women, activity rates rising as the unemployment rate falls and vice versa.

In total, the labour force is projected to rise to around 29 million by 2001, with women accounting for 46 per cent of the total. The bulk of the increase is attributable to long-term trend factors related to increasing female participation rates, particularly for those aged 25-50. It also reflects the cyclical recovery of the economy, with some previously discouraged workers (both male and female) returning to the labour market. As noted below, a large part of the increase will be people working part-time. Figure 2.2 provides the details.

Unemployment levels are expected to continue to fall in the short term as the labour market adjusts to the upturn. Unemployment peaked at just under 3 million in 1993. It is expected to fall to 2.7 million in 1994 and to 2.6 million in 1995. By the turn of the century a decline to around 2.25 million is anticipated. This remains above the level recorded in 1991.

Unemployment has fallen quite sharply in recent months but comparison with the employment figures suggests that this is primarily a function of reductions in the workforce, particularly for males. Some further reductions in unemployment are expected as the economy picks up, but these are not likely to be dramatic. As a consequence, by the year 2001 unemployment is expected to remain above 2 million despite employment rising by almost a million between 1993 and 2001. The latter represents cyclical recovery rather than long-term growth.

Changes in industrial employment

Factors influencing change
Past changes in industrial structure have arisen as a consequence of a number of inter-related factors. These include:

- technological change: as new technologies are introduced this often has the effect of reducing employment, since the same output can be produced by fewer people;

- specialisation: as economies develop there is a tendency for people and companies to specialise in particular tasks, which can result in substantial productivity gains due to increasing returns to scale and benefits from learning by doing;

- changing patterns of demand for goods and services: as economies get richer there is a tendency to follow Engel's law for individual consumption patterns, that is to spend a smaller proportion of income on necessities such as food and shelter and more on luxury items such as designer products or leisure and tourism;

- shifts in international competitiveness: these may be linked to the items above but also depend on factors such as domestic inflation rates, international exchange rates and the institutional framework for international trade (for example, membership of the European Union and GATT agreements).

The relative importance of each of these factors on developments in employment will vary from industry to industry and from one period of history to another. For example, technological change, in the form of mechanisation, was clearly a major factor in the decline of agricultural employment in the British economy after the second world war. In contrast, the decline in employment in industries such as coal mining was as much due to reduced demand for the industry's output (from other industries as well as consumers), although this in turn may have reflected technological developments in other parts of the economy. On the other hand, the collapse of UK manufacturing employment in the 1980s was related to lack of competitiveness, at least in part caused by the high exchange rate for the pound. By contrast, the growth in many service industries has reflected changing patterns of demand (such as the growth in demand for tourism and leisure) and the process of specialisation, as many new companies have been set up to subcontract work previously done within the manufacturing sector (such as cleaning, catering and many business services).

Over the next decade technological changes and competitive pressures will result in further job losses in many parts of the UK economy, most notably in manufacturing, the primary industries and utilities. However, these sorts of pressures are becoming increasingly important in many parts of the service sector as well. On a more positive note, changing patterns of demand from both producers and consumers will continue to result in rising output and employment in many parts of the service sector. Even here, however, it is easy to oversimplify. The decline of many coastal resorts is a good example. The phenomenon has reflected the fact that, although people have spent more of their higher incomes on holidays, in general this expenditure has been made abroad rather than in traditional UK holiday resorts. Some other sectors, such as air and ferry transport, have of course benefited from this.

Industrial change in the 1990s

The industrial structure of employment is expected to develop over the next 10 years in line with previous Institute assessments. Continued technological and organisational change, shifts in the patterns of demand for goods and services and changes in international comparative advantage will influence both the industrial and occupational structure of employment, as well as other aspects such as employee versus self-employed status, full-time versus part-time employment and so on.

As far as industry structure is concerned, the pattern of change is likely to show further shifts from primary and manufacturing industries to the service sector, as Figure 2.3 illustrates. This has reflected differential productivity performance, reorganisation of work (subcontracting and so on), changing patterns of final demands and many other influences. These are encapsulated, either explicitly or implicitly, in the multi-sectoral macroeconomic model used to develop the projections. Despite the dramatic shakeout of the early 1980s, the manufacturing sector has continued to lose jobs at a rapid rate in the recent recession. Almost 800,000 jobs were lost over the period 1990-94. The rate of decline has slackened in the last 12 months and a slower decline is expected over the remainder of the forecast period. Nevertheless continuing growth in productivity is expected to more than outweigh the quite buoyant output projections, resulting in a reduction to around 4 million jobs in total by 2001.

Figure 2.3 Changes in industrial employment, 1954-2001

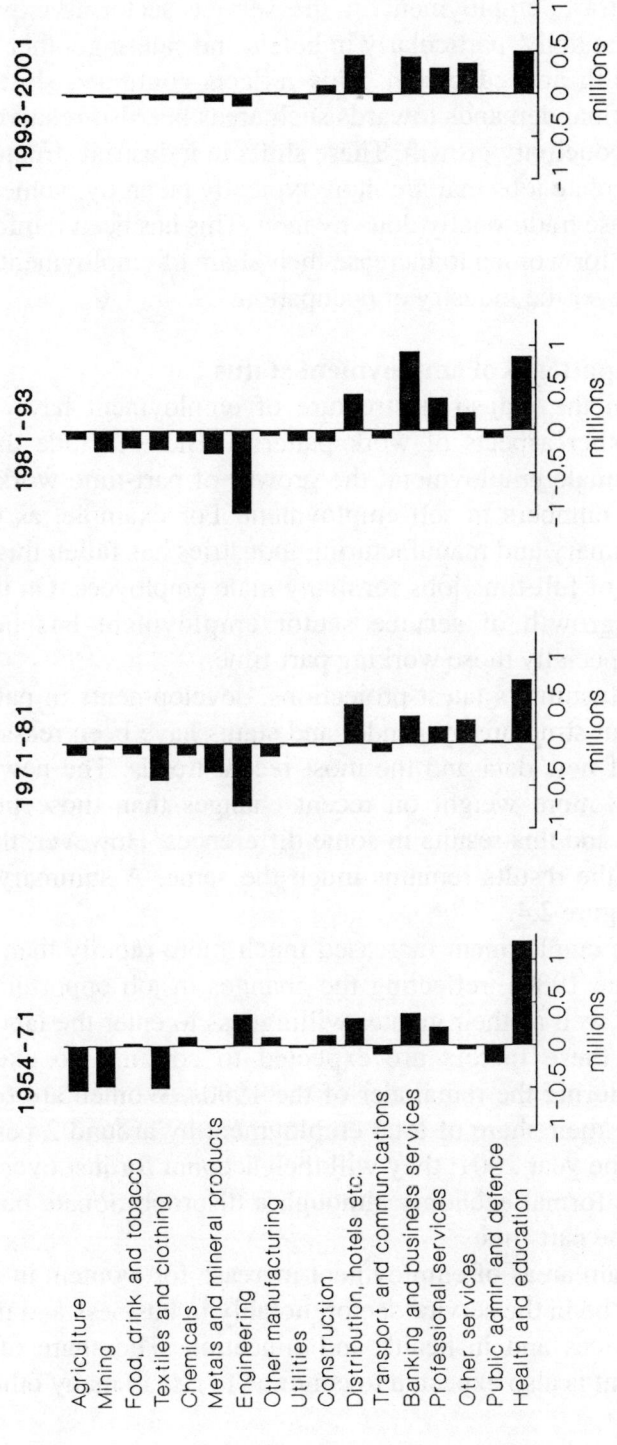

Source: IER Estimates

In contrast, employment in the service sector is expected to grow substantially, particularly in hotels and catering, other services and in health and education. This reflects continued shifts in the pattern of final demands towards such areas but also relatively slow rates of productivity growth. These shifts in industrial structure have tended to create jobs that are more typically taken by women and to remove those traditionally done by men. This has been reinforced by a tendency for women to increase their share of employment in most jobs, whatever the industry or occupation.

Changing patterns of employment status

Changes in the industrial structure of employment have also influenced other aspects of work patterns. These include the rising share of female employment, the growth of part-time working and increasing numbers in self-employment. For example, as employment in primary and manufacturing industries has fallen this has led to the loss of full-time jobs for many male employees. On the other hand the growth of service sector employment has benefited women, especially those working part-time.

In the Institute's latest projections, developments in patterns of employment structure by gender and status have been reassessed in the light of new data and the most recent trends. The new projections place more weight on recent changes than those published previously and this results in some differences. However, the broad pattern of the results remains much the same. A summary is provided in Figure 2.4.

Female employment increased much more rapidly than that for males in the 1980s, reflecting the changes in job opportunities for women, as well as their greater willingness to enter the labour market. Both these factors are expected to continue to exert their influence during the remainder of the 1990s. Women are projected to increase their share of total employment by around 2 percentage points by the year 2001; they will then account for just over half the jobs in the formal economy although a disproportionate number of these will be part-time.

The main areas of employment increase for women, in absolute terms, will be in the service sector, notably in business and miscellaneous services and in health and education. The share of female employment is also expected to continue to rise in many other areas.

Figure 2.4 Employment status

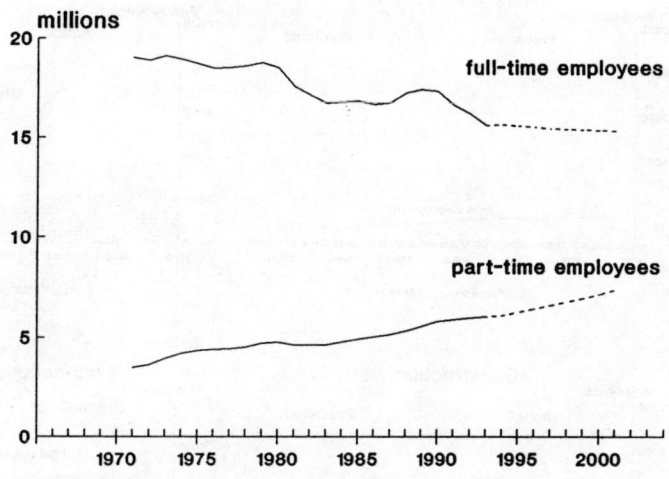

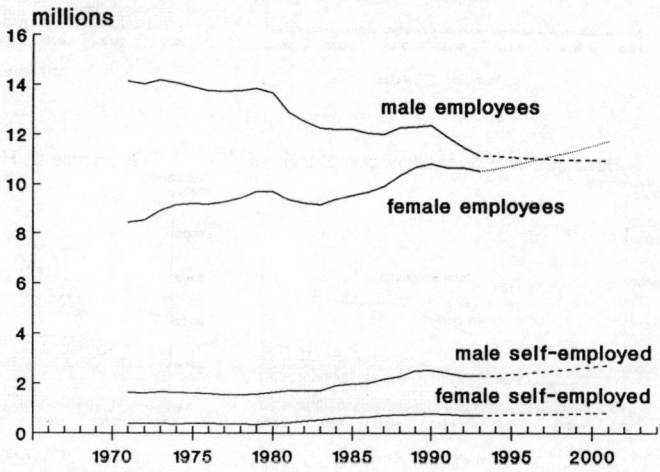

Source: IER estimates

Future skill demand and supply

Figure 2.5 Female and total employment by industry

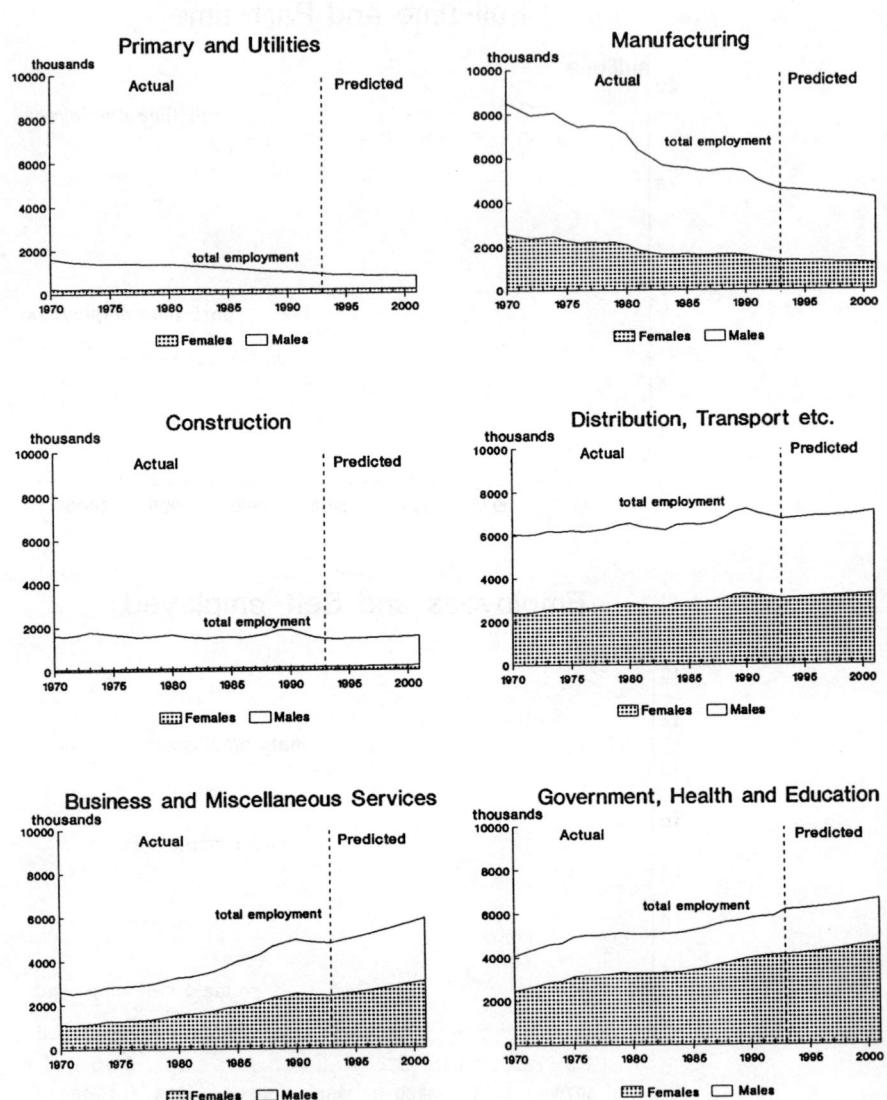

Source: IER Estimates

However, the upward trend in this share is expected to begin to flatten out in many parts of the economy as men begin, increasingly, to take on jobs in areas previously undertaken by women (for example, in distribution and other parts of the service sector). This reflects the fact that as the manufacturing sector declines there will be fewer jobs available of the kind traditionally taken by men. Figure 2.5, which compares the time profiles of female and total employment, provides the details.

For similar reasons most of the additional jobs created are likely to be part-time rather than full-time. Given their concentration in services it is also probable that a significant number will be relatively low-paid and low-status jobs. However, the trends in occupational structure in favour of the higher skilled groups, coupled with the tendency to increase the use of part-time contracts among such personnel, suggest that not all these part-time posts will be low-status ones.

Part-time employment has benefited from the growth in the service sector, and much of the observed increase in employment has reflected the greater use of this form of employment, especially within the service sector. But in recent years, part-time working has actually declined within many manufacturing industries. Part-time working can provide a very useful means of adjusting labour input to meet fluctuating demands for the service provided. The growth of part-time work has also reflected supply side pressure, especially from married women who do not want or are unable to work full-time because of family responsibilities. Part-time jobs accounted for almost all of the 1.4 million increase in employment between 1981 and 1991. The pattern in the 1990s is expected to be similar, with 1.3 million extra part-time jobs by the year 2001. Health and education services, together with other services, and distribution, hotels and so on, with increases of around 390,000, 360,000 and 460,000 jobs respectively, account for the bulk of this. Figure 2.6 illustrates the main trends in each of 6 broad sectors.

Self-employment grew rapidly in the 1980s. Over the decade 1980-90 more than a million extra people became self-employed. However, evidence from the Labour Force Survey suggest that this may have come to a halt in the early 1990s. Various explanations were advanced for why it grew so rapidly in the 1980s. Some argued that it reflected high unemployment, forcing individuals to rely on

Future skill demand and supply

Figure 2.6   Self-employment and part-time employment by industry

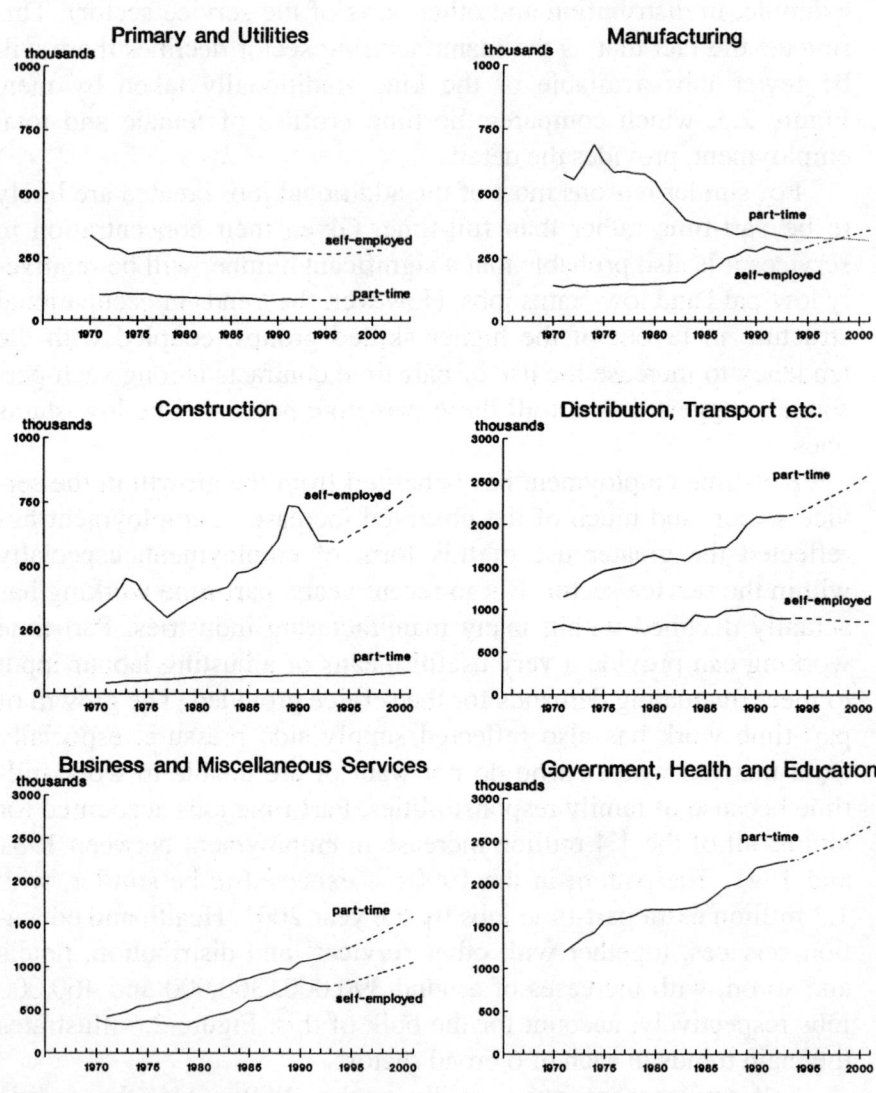

Source: IER Estimates

themselves to supply a job. If this was the case, one might have expected further increases during the 1990-92 recession, but this has not occurred. It has also been argued that the government's attempts to encourage self-reliance and enterprise were an important factor (see Johnson, 1990). Growth was heavily concentrated in construction and in certain parts of the service sector. In the case of the former much of the increase simply represented a straight switch from employee status. The recent collapse of employment in the construction industry was probably a key factor in the decline in self-employment in the early 1990s. The recession caused many self-employed persons to go out of business. The construction sector has been very hard hit, as have many small businesses in the service sector. Nevertheless, many of the factors which led to the growth during the 1980s are likely to continue to be important and the underlying trend is expected to remain upwards during the 1990s.

Self-employment is expected to continue to increase over the medium term, despite the fact that there was a decline in numbers in the early 1990s. This represented the first break in a steady upward rise for more than a decade. However, many of the factors encouraging self-employment are expected to continue to play a role and, indeed, to grow in importance over the decade. As a consequence, about 400,000 additional self-employed persons are projected between 1993 and 2001.

In the new forecasts the shares of self-employment are projected to match the increases observed in the 1980s. As a consequence, despite the recent slow-down, a further 500,000 people are expected to become self-employed by 2001. Their share of total employment is projected to increase from 12.1 to 13.4 per cent between 1993 and 2001. This phenomenon affects many industries but, as indicated in Figure 2.6, the main growth in absolute terms comes in the service sector, especially in business and miscellaneous services.

Occupational change
The analysis of changes in the occupational structure of employment can now be conducted on a firmer foundation given the publication of data from the 1991 Census of Population. The Institute has also taken the opportunity of using revised information linking the latest 1990 standard occupational classification with the old 1980 classification of occupations in order to recompile estimates of

Future skill demand and supply

Figure 2.7   Occupational employment, 1981-2001

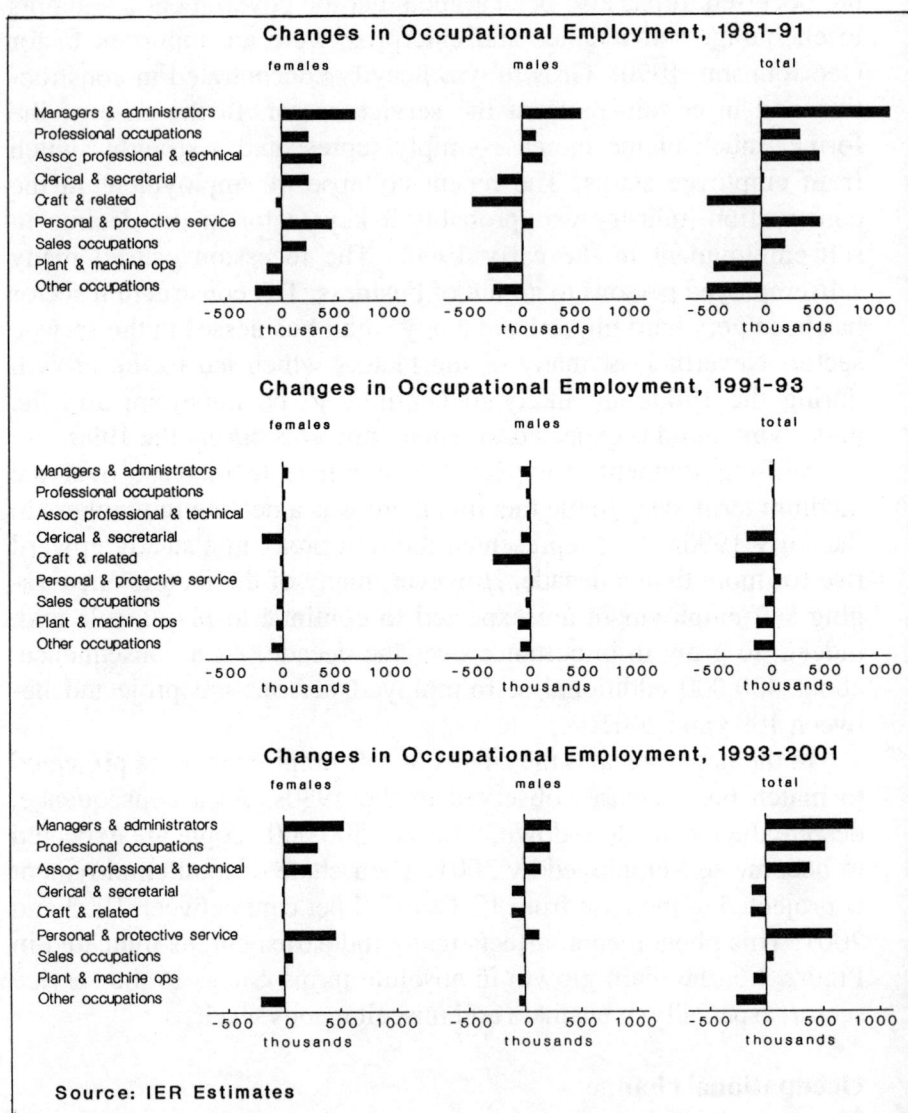

Source: IER Estimates

occupational employment on a consistent footing. The new data for 1991 and the revised 'convertor' both result in changes compared to the previous estimates of occupational structure. However, the general patterns of occupational employment and the main trends over time remain broadly the same as the previous estimates. As usual, the Census information has been complemented by data from the Labour Force Surveys although the Census data has been given precedence in assessing past and possible future trends.

The main features of change are much the same as previously projected, favouring high skills, white-collar employment (especially for women) at the expense of low-skilled, manual jobs. The recession of the early 1990s led to many redundancies among white-collar workers in some industries, especially in the south-east. Despite this, the underlying trends for such workers remain favourable and a substantial increase in the numbers in managerial, professional and associate professional jobs is expected. The outlook for those with craft skills, plant and machine operatives and unskilled labourers is much less optimistic.

The prospects for particular occupational groups are illustrated in Figures 2.7 and 2.8. An increase of about 750,000 jobs is projected for the managers and administrators category between 1993 and 2001. This may seem surprising in the light of much discussion about 'delayering' in many major companies. However the latest data suggests that such phenomena have been more than outweighed by growth in employment opportunities for such occupations elsewhere. Women are expected to see an especially large increase. Organisational and technological changes, encouraging an increasing share of these occupations in most industries (occupational effects), are more important than changes in industrial structure (industry effects) in explaining these developments.

The number of jobs for professional occupations, especially those employed in the market economy, is expected to grow rapidly. Again this primarily reflects occupational rather than industry effects. For those employed in health and education services (especially teachers) the rate of growth of public expenditure is the key factor. In total, employment in professional occupations is projected to increase by about 400,000. A similar story applies in associate professional occupations, where an overall increase of almost 400,000 is expected.

Future skill demand and supply

Figure 2.8 Major gainers and losers (changes in employment, 1993-2001)

Industry		Occupations	
Hotels and catering	(+282,000)	Corporate managers and administrators	(+592,000)
Banking, insurance and business	(+436,000)	Managers and proprietors of small businesses	(+174,000)
Professional services	(+300,000)	Science and engineering professionals	(+128,000)
Health and education	(+500,000)	Other professional occupations (accountants, lawyers etc.)	(+246,000)
Other (private) services	(+360,000)	Other associate professionals	(+295,000)
		Personal service occupations	(+523,000)
Utilities	(-57,000)	Clerical occupations	(-101,000)
Mechanical engineering	(-48,000)	Skilled engineering trades	(-135,000)
Electrical engineering	(-38,000)	Other skilled trades	(-84,000)
Food, drink and tobacco	(-52,000)	Industrial plant and machine operators	(-68,000)
Textiles and clothing	(-62,000)	Other elementary occupations (cleaners, labourers)	(-245,000)
Chemicals	(-52,000)		
Metals and mineral products	(-86,000)		
Transport and communications	(-84,000)		

Source: **Review of the Economy and Employment, 1994: Occupational Assessment**

Skill needs to the end of the century

Clerical and secretarial occupations have increased their employment very substantially over the past 30 years. Recently, this growth has slowed dramatically as the effects of new technologies have made themselves felt. Between 1991 and 1993 it is estimated that employment declined by over 250,000 for these occupations, although this was undoubtedly primarily a cyclical effect. There are now signs of falling employment shares in many industries. This trend is expected to accelerate and the prospects for the next decade are therefore for a further decrease of around 170,000 jobs.

The craft and skilled manual occupations present a mixed picture, with some growth expected for skilled construction trades from currently very depressed levels, once the economy picks up. In contrast, a modest decline is projected for skilled engineering trades as employment in engineering continues to fall despite rising output levels. The position for other skilled trades is much worse, however, and they more than account for the bulk of the projected 130,000 decline in employment in this group. Employment in these categories fell quite sharply over the recession, with some 370,000 jobs going between 1991 and 1993. Sharply falling employment in the industries employing such occupations (such as textiles), coupled with technological and other changes which are removing the need for such skills, combine to produce a continuation of past patterns of steady decline.

In contrast, the protective and personal service occupations provide a relatively bright picture. Modest growth is projected for the former category as the demand for privately provided protective services continues to rise. The main part of the projected 600,000 increase benefits the personal service occupations, many of which will be in part-time jobs. Primarily, these changes reflect the growth expected in various marketed and non-marketed services such as leisure, tourism, health and education.

Sales occupations are expected to experience only modest increases in employment over the next decade. As for the clerical and secretarial group, new technology and new methods of service delivery are resulting in substantial job cuts. The projected increase of employment in sales occupations of around 60,000 by 2001 is therefore quite modest compared to previous periods.

Plant and machine operatives face the same sort of scenario as craft and skilled manual workers. Shifts in industry structure reinforce occupational effects, resulting in a projected loss of over 100,000 jobs between 1993 and 2001. This change follows on from sharp declines which have already taken place since 1991 and represents a continuation of longer-term patterns of decline. Finally, the 'other occupations' group, comprising unskilled labourers, cleaners and so on, is also projected to experience further job losses of the order of 260,000 over the 1990s as industrial and occupational effects reinforce one another.

Implications for education and training provision

The analysis of employment structures and prospects set out above has important implications for the scale and nature of education and training provision. There are a number of key issues:

- recovery from recession;
- medium and long-term shifts in labour requirements;
- maintenance of the existing stock of skills;
- links between education and training and economic performance;
- equity versus efficiency.

Recovery from recession

The economy is now well into the recovery phase following the prolonged recession which began in 1990/91. There are already some signs of skill shortages arising in some areas. These are likely to be most serious for those industries which have been affected by the cyclical downturn such as construction and related activities and certain industries within manufacturing. However, many parts of the service sector have exhibited much greater cyclical sensitivity in recent years and these are also expected to grow rapidly in the upturn and skill shortages could also emerge here.

Labour shortages arise whenever demand exceeds supply and this may occur for a variety of reasons. In some cases it may reflect a particularly rapid growth in demand. The projections of industrial and occupational employment structure presented in this review provide some indicators of where this may happen. The expected rapid growth in employment in certain managerial, professional and associate professional categories may, for example, lead to shortages.

However, employers may also find difficulties in recruitment for other occupations where the overall demand is falling. If particular jobs are regarded as unattractive with poor job prospects this may discourage potential entrants and lead to a reduction in supply. This appears to be the case for many blue-collar, manual occupations, where past trends have indicated that long-term job opportunities are uncertain and the overall number of jobs is likely to continue to decline. Thus, despite there being a substantial continuing requirement for such occupations over the medium term, they do not appear an attractive proposition either to new entrants or indeed to many individuals already in post.

This problem may be exacerbated if employers are unable or unwilling to pay a sufficiently high wage to compensate for this uncertainty. The wage issue may also be important for some other occupations such as certain groups in the public sector, where the squeeze on public sector wages means that the pay and conditions package is not sufficiently attractive to encourage enough people to meet the notional demand. This kind of problem ranges across a broad spectrum of occupations including civil servants (both senior administrators and routine clerical staff), teachers, nurses, firemen and dustmen.

Medium and long-term shifts in labour requirements

The analysis earlier in this chapter has summarised the key features of past and projected future trends in employment structure in the UK. The overall conclusions, from the analysis of macroeconomic prospects and shifting patterns of demand for goods and services, are that the broad trends in favour of service sector employment and against employment in the primary and manufacturing sectors will continue. The latter will still remain an important engine of economic growth but this will be accompanied by rapid productivity gains so that employment will, in general, fall in industries within this sector.

Some parts of the service sector have already begun to exhibit similar features (for example, transport and communication) while others such as distribution and banking, insurance and finance are beginning to show signs of a sharp break in the previously very rapid upward trend in employment. Despite this, some increases in overall employment levels are envisaged as the economy recovers from recession. There are also important employment increases in industries such as construction (cyclical recovery) and certain other parts of the service sector (cyclical upturn plus long-term trend factors).

These medium and long-term shifts in industrial structure mean that the occupational structure of employment will continue to change in favour of white-collar, non-manual occupations, especially those with formal higher level qualifications. In contrast, the overall demand for blue-collar, manual occupations will decline.

Maintenance of the existing stock of skills

The number of people employed in a particular occupation at any point in time represents a stock of skills. The analysis above suggests how this stock may rise or decline as the pattern of demand for goods and services impinges on the demand for skills. Of course, employment only comprises one element of the total stock of skills. Some people may be unemployed, economically inactive or employed in other areas which do not use their skills directly. Nevertheless, employment is likely to provide a key indicator of the overall stock of skills.

Education and training provides a flow of newly qualified entrants to supplement this stock of skills. In order to maintain the current balance between supply and demand (or to sustain the existing degree of imbalance) this flow of new skills has to cover various requirements. It has to match the net change in total demand (which could in fact be negative). It also has to cover the losses from the existing stock due to retirements, people moving to other occupations, deaths, migration and so on. In many cases this latter requirement or 'replacement demand' will exceed the net change in total demand.

Thus, even where the total demand for a particular skill is falling, there will probably still be a need for newly qualified entrants to take the place of those retiring or leaving the stock for other reasons. Only in exceptional circumstances, such as, for example, the case of the coal mining industry over the last few years, where there is a very rapid contraction in total demand, will there be no 'replacement demand'.

This means that when looking at the overall need for education and training provision it is necessary to consider those occupations in decline as well as those projected to experience substantial growth. Unfortunately, the data necessary to produce accurate estimates of the total supply of skills and to measure replacement demand do not exist except for a few occupations. Even for those highly qualified groups where such data do exist there are major gaps and inconsistencies in the information which make an accurate assessment of replacement demand very difficult and time consuming. This does not negate the importance of the concept, however. The implication is that the projections of changes in industrial and occupational employment presented here should be regarded as providing only one indicator of where training provision priorities should be placed.

The other key element will be concerned with replacement demand. This will depend on a variety of factors which are usually only measured poorly (if at all). These include the age structure of the workforce (with implications for losses due to retirement and deaths), and information on other outflows such as occupational mobility and migration flows. However, a good indicator of the scale of such flows is available. This is, of course, the stock itself. So as well as focusing on changes in the numbers employed it is also important to consider the levels in each occupational category. Together these should give a reasonable guide as to where the main emphasis on education and training should be placed.

Links between education and training and economic performance
There is an increasing body of evidence which links investment in education and training to improved economic performance. This ranges from detailed studies of comparative training in various European countries (see, for example, Prais, 1981, 1989a and b), to much more general studies of the role of education and training in the economic growth process (such as those by Solow, 1991 and Romer, 1986 and 1987).

While such studies make a strong prima facie case for investment in education and training in order to secure and improve the long-term prospects for economic performance, they are much less helpful in providing advice on how to choose precisely what forms the education and training should take. Certain themes come through strongly, such as the need for flexibility and multiskilling, and the importance of IT-related skills. Proper accreditation recognised by both employers and individuals, is also important. The bottom line, however, is that each programme of education and training needs to be assessed on its own merits. There is no point in investing in such programmes simply in the hope that they will generate the kind of virtuous circles highlighted by Prais and Romer. Continual monitoring is necessary to ensure that the types of training being provided meet real needs. Of course, not all education (in particular) has to be justified in purely economic terms. However, if a case is being made on such grounds it is important to establish the benefits for that particular case.

Equity versus efficiency

The emphasis of the discussion above has been primarily on education and training needed to promote economic efficiency. Education and training programmes also have an important role to play in achieving equality of opportunity for those who are disadvantaged, often through no fault of their own.

The macroeconomic scenario that is likely to emerge during the late 1990s is one of continuing high levels of unemployment. The rapid structural changes occurring within the economy mean that those made redundant often have skills which are no longer suited to the needs of the modern economy. They may find it very difficult to get back into work. The long-term unemployed may therefore require special attention. Other groups such as ethnic minorities, disabled people and women may face discrimination (Lindley, 1994a). Some young people who have failed to benefit from the formal education system may also be ill-placed to compete for jobs.

In all of these cases there may be an argument for providing education and training programmes to help the individuals concerned to make a useful contribution to the wealth and welfare of the economy. Ideally this can be achieved in a manner which also promotes economic efficiency.

There is no magic formula for deriving the precise scale of provision for education and training programmes. The issues discussed here provide some pointers as to where the emphasis should lie and where changes may be required. This information needs to be used in conjunction with other evidence, such as the perceptions of those directly involved about the degree to which existing provision is meeting current needs, and any other qualitative indicators of how things are changing 'on the ground'.

The key considerations are:

- the current stock of skills (that is, total numbers employed in each occupation): this gives an indicator of what replacement demand requirements might be;
- net changes in total demand: this provides an indicator of where the forces of demand and supply for commodities are causing growth or decline in the need for particular skills;
- target groups: the long-term unemployed, young people, ethnic minorities and some women may face particular problems in entering or returning to the labour market. Special emphasis may be required on these target groups.

References

Barker T S and A W A Peterson (1987) *The Cambridge Multisectoral Dynamic Model of the British Economy*. Cambridge: Cambridge University Press

Briscoe G and R A Wilson (1991) 'Explanations of the Demand for Labour in the United Kingdom Engineering Sector'. *Applied Economics* 23, pp.913-926

Cambridge Econometrics (1994) *Industry and the British Economy: Analysis and Forecasts to 2005*. Autumn Report. Cambridge: Cambridge Econometrics

Department of Employment (1994) 'British Labour Force Projections: 1994 to 2006'. *Employment Gazette*, pp.111-121

Greenhalgh C A, B Suer, P Taylor and R A Wilson (1992) 'Trade Performance and Innovatory Activity: A Review'. In *External Imbalances and Policy Constraints in the 1990s*. ed. C Milner and N Snowden, pp.91-123. London: Macmillan

Greenhalgh C A, P Taylor and R A Wilson (1994) 'Innovation and Export Volumes and Prices – a disaggregated study'. *Oxford Economic Papers*, 46, pp.102-134

Institute for Employment Research (1993) *Review of the Economy and Employment: Occupational Assessment, 1992/3*. Coventry: University of Warwick

Institute for Employment Research (1994) *Review of the Economy and Employment: Occupational Assessment, 1994*. Coventry: University of Warwick

Johnson S (1990) *The Small Firms Sector: Review of the Economy and Employment, 1990 – Volume 1*. Coventry: Institute for Employment Research, University of Warwick

Lindley R (1994a) (ed.) *Labour Market Structures and Policies for Women.* Manchester: EOC

Lindley R (1994b) 'A Perspective on IER Forecasting Activities and Future Developments'. Fifth Anniversary Symposium, Researchcentrum voor Onderwijs en Arbeidsmarkt: Rijksuniversiteit Limburg, Maastricht, May. In *Labour Market Forecasts by Occupation and Education,* ed. H Heijke. Massachusetts, USA: Kluwer Academic Press

Neale A J and R A Wilson (1987) 'Average Weekly Hours of Work in the United Kingdom, 1948-80: A Disaggregated Analysis'. In *Working Below Capacity,* ed. D L Bosworth and D F Heathfield (1987), Chapter 9. London: Macmillan.

Prais, S J (1981) 'Vocational Qualifications of the Labour Force in Britain and Germany'. *National Institute Economic Review* 98, pp.47-59

Prais, S J (1989a) 'Qualified Manpower in Engineering'. *National Institute Economic Review* February, pp.76-83

Prais, S J (ed.) (1989b) *Productivity, Education and Training.* London: National Institute of Economic and Social Research

Romer, P M (1986) 'Increasing Returns and Long-run Growth'. *Journal of Political Economy* 94, pp.1002-1037

Romer, P M (1987) 'Growth Based on Increasing Returns due to Specialisation'. *American Economic Review,* Papers and Proceedings, vol. 77, pp.56-62

Solow, R M (1991) 'Growth Theory'. In *Companion to Contemporary Economic Thought,* ed. D Greenaway, M Bleamey and I Stewart. London: Routledge

Wilson R A (1994) 'Modelling and Forecasting the Structure of Employment in the UK'. Fifth Anniversary Symposium, Researchcentrum voor Onderwijs en Arbeidsmarkt: Rijksunivsiteit Limburg, Maastricht, May. In *Labour Market Forecasts by Occupation and Education,* ed. H Heijke. Massachusetts, USA: Kluwer Academic Press

Notes

1. This paper is based on results from the Institute's *Review of the Economy and Employment, 1994: Occupational Assessment,* to which the reader is referred for further details. This work was funded by the former Employment Department. The author is also grateful to colleagues at the Institute and Cambridge Egonometrics for their assistance. However, they bear no responsibilities for the views expressed or any remaining errors.

2. The Institute's approach to labour market assessments is set out in Lindley (1994) and Wilson (1994). Further details about the macroeconomic model may be found in Barker and Petersen (1987) and Cambridge Econometrics (1994). Some of the Institute's contributions to model development may be found in Briscoe and Wilson (1991), Greenhalgh *et al* (1992 and 1994) and Neale and Wilson (1987).

3 Graduates: shortage or glut?

Helen Connor

Is there really a glut of graduates in the UK? Are we producing too many for the needs of the UK economy? Or is it that the current problems of supply exceeding demand are still mainly due to the effects of the prolonged recession? Will problems of shortages start to re-emerge once the recovery begins in earnest, as happened in the 1980s?

At first glance there appear to be several messages coming from the graduate market at present which can be confusing to employers and prospective students alike. On the one hand there is evidence that we have more than enough graduates: for example, employers being overwhelmed with applications for graduate vacancies, an average of 90 per vacancy (AGR, 1994); graduates having to make many applications to succeed in getting a job; and continuing high levels of graduate unemployment, over 11 per cent. On the other hand, we hear from some employers about shortages and recruitment difficulties; not widespread or general difficulties but in specific areas. For example, concerns from employers about mismatches between skills sought and those available in applicants; a lack of good quality engineers; and rising salary levels in parts of the market (particularly the top end).

The likelihood is that there will be a glut of graduates in general as well as selected shortages for the foreseeable future. This is a new situation which differs from the 1980s post-recessionary period when shortages started to emerge as demand expanded rapidly. This chapter explores this further and examines the reasons for it. It looks at trends in both the supply and the demand for graduates, highlighting particular issues of increasing diversity within the higher education system, the broadening of the graduate market and employer concerns about skill deficiencies.

Recent trends

From the perspectives of both potential students (and their parents, teachers and career advisers) and employers, the signals given out by the shifts in the graduate market and government policy can appear inconsistent and paradoxical.

First, the graduate market has been very volatile, with several periods of boom and slack over the last 20 years, following the swings in the economic cycle. As shown in Figure 3.1, graduate unemployment has, with a slight lag, closely followed a mirror image of economic growth. The most recent swing in fortunes came in 1990, when the graduate market moved quickly from a situation of increasing demand outstripping available supply to one of cutbacks in vacancies for new graduates, with even some redundancies among recent recruits, and intense competition for the available jobs (Connor, Court and Jagger, 1993). Between 1989 and 1992 the unemployment rate for graduates more than doubled to almost 12 per cent.

Figure 3.1 Real GDP growth and graduate unemployment

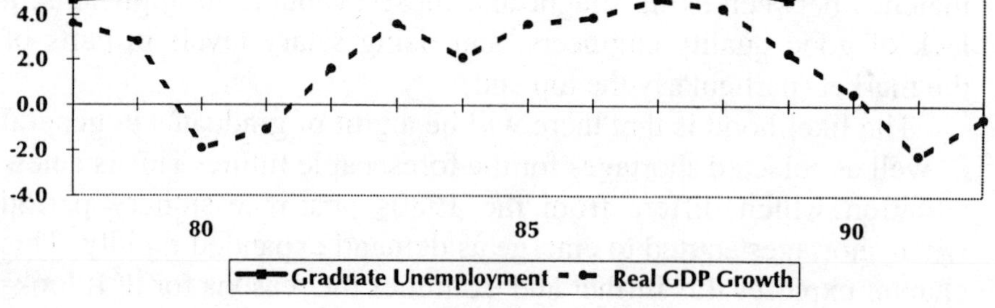

Source: IES/OECD/USR

Just at this time, when demand was at a periodic low, there was a rapid rise in supply of graduates. The expansion in the UK higher education system came about because of a relaxation of government expenditure restrictions in 1989 and encouragement to increase the education participation rates of young people (Baker, 1989). There has also been a significant growth in participation by older people and non-A level qualified entrants encouraged by the introduction of access courses and a greater vocational dimension in university courses. There are now 50 per cent more first degree graduates being produced than five years ago.

It is not surprising therefore that many of today's graduates are experiencing difficulties in the labour market. Supply is so much greater than in the past and demand is only just beginning to pick up again. The latest figures from the Association of Graduate Recruiters (AGR) biennial surveys of salaries and vacancies which are undertaken by the Institute for Employment Studies (IES) showed a 10 per cent increase in vacancies for graduates between 1993 and 1994, the first real growth for some years, and a similar rise was forecast for the coming year.

However, within this overall picture of growth in supply and still relatively depressed demand, there is evidence of some shortages existing which have become more pronounced of late. The number of employers reporting shortfalls in recruitment has been increasing (AGR, 1994). Over one in five of the graduate recruiters surveyed by IES in 1994 reported shortages in specific areas, up from just 12 per cent a year ago. This still compares very favourably with the situation five years ago when large numbers of employers were complaining of shortages, but it is still a surprisingly high number today. Industrial employers were experiencing greater difficulties, 28 per cent in 1994 compared to 18 per cent the previous year. The specific areas mentioned most often were engineering and electronics disciplines, and financial, accountancy, sales and marketing posts. There is also increasing market competition as demonstrated by higher than average annual salary increases (see, for example, AGR/Court and Jagger, 1995).

Education expansion and the economy
Last year's Competitiveness White Paper (DTI, 1994) emphasised the link between high-level skills and competitiveness and high-

lighted the crucial role of higher education as a source of managerial and professional staff. The government is committed to maintaining a high output of graduates, though the growth rates experienced in the last five years are unlikely to be repeated in the next, partly on expenditure grounds. The Confederation of British Industry (CBI), however, has also called for more graduate output (CBI, 1994). It recommended that the UK move to a more demand-led system of higher education, and that restricting access to the higher education system to just over 30 per cent of young people in the UK would not help competitiveness in the global economy. It recommended a rise in output so that a minimum of 40 per cent of young people graduate by 2000, though the report did not discuss in any detail what effect this expansion would have on the labour market.

Do we need more graduates? At a time when we have a significant number of new graduates unemployed, the traditional argument that more graduates need to be produced to fuel economic growth and match our international competitors (which was put forward as a reason for expansion in the late 1980s) does not now meet with the general acceptance and support that it used to. Several researchers have been looking more critically at the economic arguments (Murphy, 1993) and have suggested that Britain has consistently overstated its requirements for graduates and the significance of their role in increasing international competitiveness.

On the other hand, many competitor countries believe more firmly than here in the UK that the education and training of a significant proportion of the population to higher levels will provide the greatest benefit to an upgrading economy (Porter, 1990). Furthermore, while international comparisons show that the UK's graduation rate now compares favourably with many economic competitor countries, and we have one of the highest proportions of young people becoming graduates (OECD, 1993), our competitors are not standing still. For example, newly industrialised countries like South Korea already have more students in higher education than the UK's target for 2000 (at 35 per cent). A 1990 survey showed that more than 80 per cent of South Korean parents expect their children to be in higher education in the next decade which gives an indication of the likely pace of international developments (Finegold, 1993).

The belief that a better educated society is a better society is likely to continue to receive general support, but it would seem that there is a need to look much more closely at the link between continued investment growth in higher education and economic prosperity, especially in the light of the trend towards mass higher education and the growth of graduate employment in areas not considered suitable 10 or 15 years ago.

Diversity
One of the reasons for the paradoxes that currently exist in the graduate market and for the lack of consensus about future needs, is the increasing diversity in both the higher education system and the student population and in the employment opportunities available to graduates.

By 1995 the output from higher education will have increased by over 50 per cent since 1990 to around 200,000 per year. The economy has had to absorb a very high increase in the number of qualified individuals: almost 700,000 first degree students graduated between 1988 and 1992, and not all will have entered employment areas traditionally associated with graduates. Indeed, as discussed further below there is a growing body of evidence that many graduates are taking jobs where their degree is not required.

Within this overall growth, the characteristics of the undergraduate population have changed significantly. There are now more women, particularly older women, participating in higher education (Figure 3.2). The percentage of entrants who are male, under 21 year-olds has reduced from 49 per cent in 1987 to 38 per cent in 1993. There are more students entering with qualifications other than A levels: 27 per cent of those admitted through UCCA/PCAS in 1993 had either a vocational (for example, BTEC) or access qualifications or no formal qualifications at all, and in engineering and technology the percentage was as high as 41 per cent. In addition, today's students are experiencing a different HE system and, possibly, a different learning environment from those of 10 or 20 years ago. More modularised courses, the removal of the binary line, growth in vocational courses, work-based learning and assessment are a few of the many initiatives which have recently been introduced. The result is a more diverse student population and more variations in quality of output from university to university, course

Future skill demand and supply

Figure 3.2 UCCA and PCAS home admissions to full-time and sandwich first degree courses by age and sex, 1987-1993

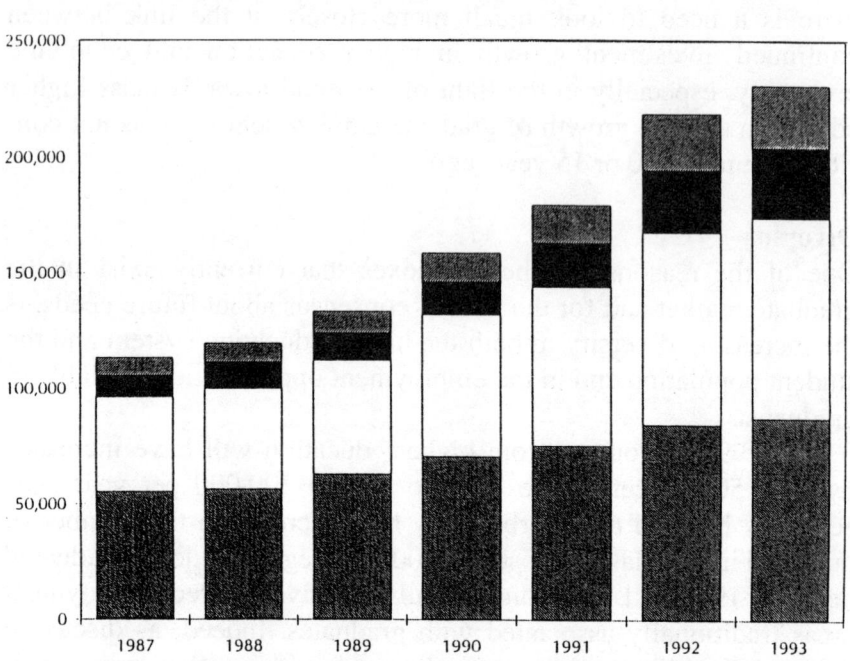

Source: IES/UCCA/PCAS

to course. Thus, it is not surprising that it is becomingly increasingly difficult to generalise about supply trends and the experiences of some students entering the employment market can be quite different from others.

Turning to the demand side a much higher proportion of today's first degree graduates go on to postgraduate study than ten years ago, and there are many more places available – it has been a faster growing sector than first degree study – partly because of the recession, as an alternative to being unemployed, but mainly because more professions are seeking postgraduate qualifications for professional practice, for example, lawyers, teachers, social workers. The value of a postgraduate qualification is also recognised more in management (for example, MBAs) and technical jobs (for example, in IT).

The distribution of graduates among employment sectors has changed markedly in the last ten years: many more graduates enter the services sector and a lower proportion go to industry than previously. In particular, there has been considerable growth in the recruitment of graduates in retail and financial services. Graduates are also entering a different range of jobs. Some are jobs which previously did not require a degree on entry but now do, for instance many of the professions, the retail sector (for example, store management), publishing or the media; while others are jobs which do not necessarily require a degree but graduates often have the advantage over less qualified people such as A level holders (who are less numerous anyway). Thus we have graduates displacing less qualified people and often doing jobs below their capabilities.

Evidence of greater fragmentation in the graduate market can be seen in the greater differentiation developing between the top and bottom ends, as seen in starting salaries. The top 10 per cent of graduate recruiters (that is those with identified graduate vacancies or graduate training programmes) are paying starting salaries for first degree graduates of over £17,000, while there is a much larger number clustering around £12,000 or under. The former tend to be mainly City-based with professional training profiles (for example, in law, underwriting, investment banking) and compete fiercely for the 'cream of the crop'.

Further evidence of a broadening of the graduate market is shown in the 1991 Census data (Qualified Manpower Tables) (OPCS, 1994). Degree level qualified people are spread across a range of managerial, administrative, professional and associated professional occupations, but 12 per cent of employees in other occupations are also graduates. There is a lack of substantial statistical evidence on graduate underutilisation from employers. Much of it is anecdotal or based on small samples from particular universities or courses. The recent major graduate follow-up survey by Brennan and McGeevor (1993) provides some of the best evidence to date from graduates. It showed that 34 per cent of them viewed they were overqualified for their job and 43 per cent felt their work did not require graduate ability.

But does this really matter? There is no agreed definition of underutilisation or what is a 'graduate job'. It is not set in tablets of stone, it is a dynamic thing which is constantly changing as the nature of jobs changes and as the available skills to fill them change too. But it does matter in at least one important way. If there is a serious mismatch between expectations and reality, and if graduates are disappointed about the end result of their studies, they may become disillusioned about the value of education. In a similar way, their parents, many of whom are now paying out large sums to support their children at university, will ask: was it all worth it? It may also start to be a concern if perceived rates of return from education fall with lower starting salaries and subsequent lower career trajectories, thus possibly discouraging people from entering higher education in the first place.

Skill deficiencies
Another emerging key issue in the graduate labour market is the growing dissatisfaction of employers with the abilities and skills of the majority of graduate applicants. The June 1994 AGR survey showed that the skills in short supply were mainly in business awareness and communication, followed by leadership and team working (Table 3.1). These are skills which employers have consistently highlighted as being crucial to their future success in other surveys (see for example, Harvey and Green, 1993; AGR, 1993; Engineering Council, 1993), and which they have difficulty in finding. It is usually a combination of technical and personal skills which is in most demand. Thus it is of little use increasing the number of engineers produced if the academic quality is not high enough nor their personal skills adequate for the changing business world they are entering.

The June 1994 AGR survey results can be compared with a similar question in 1991, and it is clear that there is now a greater awareness among employers of personal transferable skills. Employers are seeking graduates with a broader range of skills and abilities than academic qualifications alone. Communication skills and team working are increasingly demanded while specific knowledge of discipline is not perceived as so much of a problem as in 1991.

There are several explanations for this trend. First, there is a greater need to work more closely with the customer and for more customer orientation and fewer 'back room' positions: the 'customer is king' as recently highlighted by the Engineering Council in their

Table 3.1
Skill shortages by order of importance

	Total*	Most important %	Second most imp. %	Third most imp. %
Communication skills	63.3	24.3	22.0	19.7
Business awareness	62.7	24.8	18.2	19.7
Ability to work in a team	30.1	8.4	10.5	11.2
Leadership	27.9	9.7	8.6	9.6
Problem solving	27.5	4.0	9.1	14.4
Knowledge and competence in discipline	18.0	7.5	5.7	4.8
Conceptual ability	17.0	4.4	5.7	6.9
Numeracy	14.8	4.4	7.2	3.2
Foreign languages	14.0	1.8	5.3	6.9
Good general education	12.3	5.3	3.8	3.2
Other skills	8.4	4.9	2.4	1.1
Computer literacy	3.9	0.4	1.4	2.1
Base:	–	226	209	188

* The total column is the sum of the most important, second most important and third most important columns and provides an indication of the overall importance ascribed to each skill by employees.

proposals for changes to engineering formation (Engineering Council, 1995). Second, there is the changing operational structure of many companies, which put more emphasis on teamworking and which have less hierarchical structures, and thus place greater emphasis on the requirement for good communication skills. Third, and this is unproved, it may be that as the supply of graduates increases some employers can afford to be more choosy and have increased their entry standards accordingly.

How can graduates best develop the skills that business identifies as being deficient and which needs in larger quantity? Initiatives such as Enterprise in Higher Education (EHE) are designed to bring academics and industrialists together to help prepare students for work, but in terms of coverage their impact is still quite small. Not all academics see that developing personal skills should be high on their agenda, or even on the agenda at all. The solutions may lie more outside higher education in the provision of good quality work experience for young people, or further back in their school education. But higher education has some responsibility for developing these 'work relevant' skills and there is a need for a more integrated approach to be taken across the curriculum, and greater interaction between employers and universities.

Future outlook

Looking to the future, it is clear that on the supply side further growth in entry to higher education is going to be curtailed by the government until at least 1997. There is likely to be a 27 per cent increase in output between 1993 and 1997, with the peak coming in 1996. Beyond then, the output is likely to remain fairly stable. Demand is starting to pick up among the main (mostly large) graduate recruiting companies and showing more consistent, though modest, growth than for some time, though unlikely to return to pre-1990 levels. Growth in graduate recruitment in smaller firms is also apparent, but is being constrained by the shorter-term resourcing plans of many small employers and their lack of conviction over the benefits of taking a graduate recruit. Graduates may have to adopt a different job-search strategy if they are to make significant inroads into this market, by making more speculative applications, applying for more generally advertised jobs and using networks. There may also need to be more direct initiatives taken by careers advisers, government, TECs or other bodies to encourage greater use and awareness of graduates by smaller firms.

Despite the uncertainties in the graduate market, all the signs seem to point to both rising demand and rising supply over the next five years. Supply is still likely to outpace demand overall, however, despite the slowdown in new graduate output growth, because of two further factors: a large pool of graduates who have delayed their job search by taking postgraduate study, a year abroad or simply a lower-level temporary job; and those unemployed from previous years still seeking their first job. These 'late entrants' will inflate the supply figures for some years to come. The recovery in the graduate job market is happening more slowly than forecast and it will take a more significant economic upturn than forecast to bring the market more into balance with supply. An ameliorating factor in all of this will be the pace of change in graduates' own expectations of what is a 'suitable' job and the extent to which employers, especially those who have not traditionally recruited graduates, recognise and utilise the pool of graduate talent. At the same time, the current difficulties of skills mismatch between employer requirements and those available in graduate recruits will not have gone away and may even get worse unless more steps are taken to increase opportunities for students to gain work experience and to develop their personal skills.

With the current changes in higher education, particularly its greater accessibility, the opening up of new learning methods and the attention given to quality standards, we have the opportunity in the UK for a much larger number of people to benefit from higher education than in the past. The system is in place, though under considerable financial pressure. It is important to ensure that too many people do not see their degree as a waste because of problems in finding a job afterwards. Nor should the quality of an undergraduate education be diluted by putting excess pressure on the system and thus failing to produce the graduates in sufficient numbers with the right kinds of skills that the economy needs and wants. This will be the challenge for the next decade.

References

Association of Graduate Recruiters (1993) *Roles for Graduates in the 21st Century.* London: AGR

Association of Graduate Recruiters (1994) *Graduate Salary and Vacancies Survey,* Summer update. June 1994. London: AGR

Association of Graduate Recruiters (1995) *Graduate Salary and Vacancies.* January 1995. AGR

Baker K (1989) 'Higher Education 25 years on'. *Policy Studies,* 9

Brennan J and P McGeevor (1993) *Students, Courses and Jobs: The relationship between Higher Education and the Labour Market.* London: Jessica Kingsley

Confederation of British Industry (1994) 'Thinking Ahead: Ensuring the Expansion of Higher Education into the 21st Century'. June 1994. CBI

Connor H, G Court and N Jagger (1993) *The IMS Graduate Review 1993.* Institute of Manpower Studies (now IES), Report No 252

Connor H, G Court and N Jagger (1994) *The IES Graduate Review 1994.* Institute for Employment Studies, Report No 278

Department of Trade and Industry (1994) *Competitiveness White Paper.* June 1994. London: HMSO

Engineering Council (1993) *A review of future engineering skill needs of UK industry.* A report to the Engineering Council by Paul Hendry and co.

Engineering Council (1995) *Competence and Commitment.* January 1995. London: Engineering Council

Finegold D (1993) 'The emerging post-16 system: analysis and change'. In *The Reform of the Post-17 Education and Training System in England and Wales.* London: Longman

Harvey L and D Green (1993) *Employer Satisfaction, Report on the Quality in Higher Education project.* University of Central England

Murphy K (1993) 'A degree of Waste: the economic benefits of educational expansion', *Oxford Review of Education,* vol.19, no.1

OECD (1993) *Education at a Glance.* Paris: OECD

OPCS (1994) *Census of Population 1991: Qualified Manpower Reports.* London: HMSO

Porter M (1990) *The Competitive Advantage of Nations.* London: Macmillan

4 As the labour market for scientists and technologists becomes more international, do we need to train more?

Richard Pearson

There are many indicators of economic well-being and competitiveness. The precise position of the UK in the international 'league tables' depends on the indicator being used; that the UK is no longer the leading economic nation is not, however, in question. For example, a recent European Commission report (EC,1994) suggests that the UK is ranked eighth in Europe in terms of per capita GDP with the newly emerging Pacific nations catching up fast.

The availability and use of skilled personnel are widely regarded as key ingredients for the competitiveness of companies and nations (Porter, 1990). The development and use of science and technology (S&T) skills are seen as a crucial subset of the needs of a technologically-based economy. For example, investment in education and training, both in general and in science and technology, is seen as an important factor in the rapid economic emergence of the Pacific countries such as Japan, Korea and Taiwan (Woods, 1994). The United States is also seen as drawing on a strong S&T base to underpin its strong economic performance and development. That S&T alone is not enough to guarantee success is shown by the lack of economic development in much of the old Soviet empire where large numbers of S&Ts were employed and are now unemployed.

The lead times to develop scientists and technologists are long, the costs high and the benefits uncertain. All of this makes any form of 'planning' or looking forward both more desirable and at the same time more difficult. Planning or even anticipating needs and trends is made even more difficult by the fact that the increasing transferability of technology and globalisation of research and development (R&D) means that many organisations are now seeking to resource key activities from the international marketplace; as a consequence no country or company can insulate itself from broader global trends.

If employing organisations and policy bodies are to take effective decisions about the recruitment, development and employment of such potentially internationally mobile staff, and long-term education and training strategies are to be developed, then there is a need for better information about the relative availability, supply and flows of these people, both now and as they are expected to develop over the coming years.

A key question for policy-makers, then, is whether intervention is needed to boost further the UK's supply of higher level S&T skills to aid competitiveness, copying the example of Japan, Korea and other Pacific-rim countries over the last two decades, or whether market forces will bring about any necessary changes in the availability of such skills as has been the case in the US.

The purpose of this chapter is to place the availability and use of human resources in science and technology (HRST) in the UK in an international context and to explore the extent to which the supply of S&T skills needs increasing to help boost competitiveness.

Background

The UK has had a long history of concern and debate about its lack of skills, in terms of both quantity and quality. In the case of scientists and technologists this concern goes back more than a century (Weiner,1981). Much of the concern in science and technology has centred on the apparent shortage of higher-level skills, particularly for engineers (Pearson, 1989), although more recently this concern has widened to include intermediate and lower-level skills.

There are many influences on the balance between the supply and demand for skills. On the demand side, economic, technological and organisational change has led both to new jobs emerging and to old ones disappearing. On balance the number of science-related jobs has been growing over the last two decades and is expected to grow by more than 20 per cent over the decade to 2000, the fastest growing occupational group in the UK (IER,1994), this growth mirroring trends in other industrialised economies.

Supply-side influences include demographic factors, which in the mid-1980s were (as it turns out, wrongly) expected to lead to a significant downturn in the demand for places in higher education, as well as educational, economic, social and cultural factors. For example, engineering has been said to be unattractive to would-be students because of its low public esteem in the UK in comparison with the other professions such as law and accountancy. Then, in the late 1980s, the City was blamed for supposedly creaming off the best engineering graduates to the detriment of the engineering industry. The data, however, shows that this was not the case, with the vast majority of engineering graduates entering engineering-related employment soon after their graduation while the numbers going into the finance sector, although growing, remained tiny (Pearson, 1989).

Despite the concerns of the 1980s, the supply of science and engineering graduates has boomed over the last decade with the growth continuing. For example, the number of students graduating in engineering will have grown by nearly 50 per cent between 1990 and 1995 and those in the sciences by more than 50 per cent over this period (although the growth rate across all disciplines will have been nearly 75 per cent over the same period). Unemployment and underemployment have been affecting all types of graduates, with the unemployment rate six months after graduation for those in the sciences reaching 13 per cent last year compared with 12 per cent for engineering graduates, both figures above the average for all graduates of just under 12 per cent (Court et al., 1994a).

The rapid expansion of higher education has lead to some concern that the UK may be following the experiences of the US which expanded its HE system some years ago. In the United States the rapid expansion in supply has, despite an expanding job market, been followed by declining real starting salaries for new graduates: in 1990 they were 16 per cent lower than in 1969; one in five graduates was classified as being in a job where they are under-utilised; the time taken to find a job has lengthened considerably; and employers were increasingly looking for graduates with work experience and were using short-term assignments and placements as part of their recruitment and screening processes (Court et al., 1994b). The UK seems increasingly to be following these patterns which look to be long-lasting and are expected to continue even with an upturn in graduate recruitment post-recession.

Table 4.1
Main reasons for recruiting foreign nationals

	Very important
Need for specific technical/scientific expertise	71
Development of an international culture	56
Changes in international collaboration	56
Availability of non-national staff	49
Availability of national staff	42
Changes in R&D staff mobility	27
Changes in size of research centre	34
EU programmes e.g. ESPRIT, RACE	33

n=105

Source: Court, 1994c

One particular recent development affecting scientists and technologists has been the growing internationalisation of the markets for both S&T services and skills (science based products having had an international market for many years). An example of the former is the transfer of high-level computing and software jobs to India and to other less developed economies where skill levels are high and wages low, with technology, in the form of satellites, allowing interactive contact with client sites in north America and Europe.

An example of the way the labour market for scientists and technologists is internationalising is shown by the R&D industry. Among 100 key R&D centres across Europe, on average 10 per cent of scientists are now foreign nationals and as many as 30 per cent are in the small, R&D intensive countries such as the Netherlands and Switzerland. The main reasons for recruiting foreign nationals have been the requirement for specialist skills, lack of local specialists and the desire to build an international culture in the organisation. Salary differentials have not been a significant reason (Table 4.1). Recruitment has often flowed from international collaborative projects and visiting fellowships, while personal contacts, recommendations and advertisements have also been important. The United States and China were numerically the most important indi-

Table 4.2
Recruitment sources, the most important countries

	Mentions	Total recruits
USA	21	156
China	13	113
France	21	100
United Kingdom	24	94
Germany	14	81
Eastern Europe inc USSR	17	61
Other Europe	38	170
Other	25	56
Japan	4	59
n=105		

Source: Court, 1994c

vidual sources of recruits followed by France, the UK, Germany and Japan. Eastern Europe and inter-EU mobility have also been important (Table 4.2). Looking ahead, one in four expected to increase their employment of foreign nationals in the coming years (Court et al, 1994c).

The UK's strong track record in science and technology and the widespread use of the English language mean that the UK is a key part of this international labour market with a 'brain drain' of personnel moving in and out of the country, and the UK providing an attractive location for R&D.

International comparisons
The first global report on S&T Indicators, (EC, 1994) seeks to address the paucity of internationally available data against which countries can benchmark themselves, and policy-makers assess international S&T issues.

In any international analysis of HRST it is important to recognise that while there may be a common language this conceals some fundamental cultural differences as to the nature of S&T. Thus in the traditional Anglo-Saxon culture S&T means science and technology and engineering, with an occasional recognition that the social sciences are borderline 'science' subjects. By way of contrast, in continental Europe the concept of 'science' embraces all intellectual activity, and the term scientist will include those working in the humanities (Pearson, 1994). There are, of course, as many differences between the labour markets for different types of scientists and technologists, for example, electronic engineers and zoologists, as there are between the sciences and the humanities.

Another contrast lies in the fact that the typical UK graduate is aged 21 or 22 and will have studied on a three or four year degree programme with only a small proportion of the entrants dropping out. On the continent the degree courses are typically much longer, four to six years, there are much higher drop-out rates and graduates are often aged 26 or more on graduation. Therefore one has to use great caution when comparisons are made about UK and continental graduate scientists and technologists.

Looking internationally, the US dominates in terms of the number of science and technology students (using the narrower Anglo-Saxon definition) graduating each year (over 250,000), matching the total for all of the EU countries, with Japan following with just over 100,000. However, when we look at the figures on a national, per capita basis we see a more even picture, with the UK graduation rate exceeding that of the United States and Japan, well ahead of Germany and Italy and slightly behind that of France (Figure 4.1). What

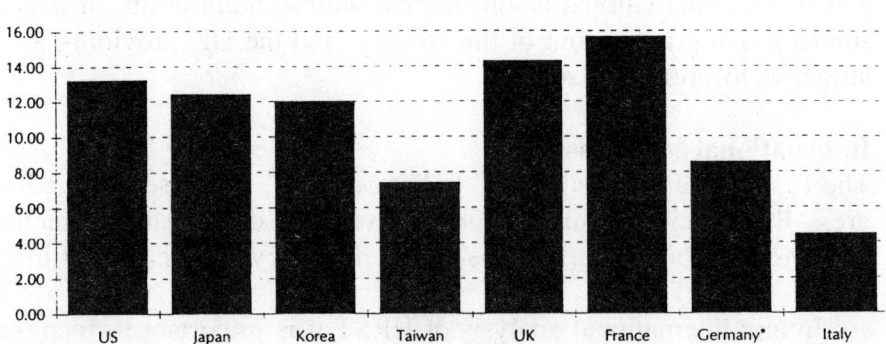

Figure 4.1 NSE graduates per 1,000 20-24 year olds

Do we need to train more?

Figure 4.2   Engineering and technology graduates per 1,000 20-24 year olds

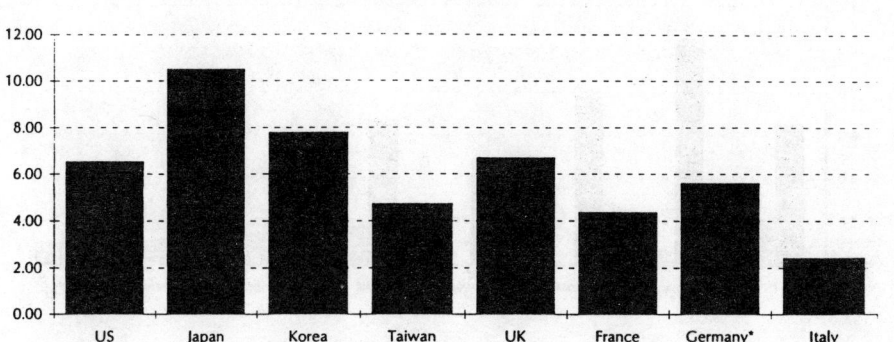

is noticeable is the scale of the output in Korea and Taiwan. Both the newly emerging Pacific nations have benefited from extremely rapid growth in their output of such graduates while the numbers in the US and Japan have barely changed in recent years. Growth in the UK, France and Germany during the 1980s has been between 20 per cent and 60 per cent.

In the more focused area of engineering, a discipline that has been of particular concern in the UK, it can be seen that the US and Japan dominate in terms of the numbers graduating, but that in terms of per capita output the figures are more evenly matched, with Japan and Korea leading, closely followed by the US and the UK (Figure 4.2). Again, the most rapid growth rates are to be found in Korea followed, interestingly, by the UK and Germany and with graduate numbers in engineering barely growing in the US and Japan.

Another interesting insight is the fact that while women are significantly under-represented in the supply of new engineering graduates in all of the main economies, their representation in the UK is among the best, with the United States leading, Germany following and Japan trailing well behind (Figure 4.3).

The available evidence suggests then that the UK is not significantly lagging in its supply of S&Ts. But what of the use made of them? Here, unfortunately, there are major problems in defining occupations (Pearson, 1994), so use is made of the data on employ-

Future skill demand and supply

Figure 4.3 Total and female engineering and technology graduation rates

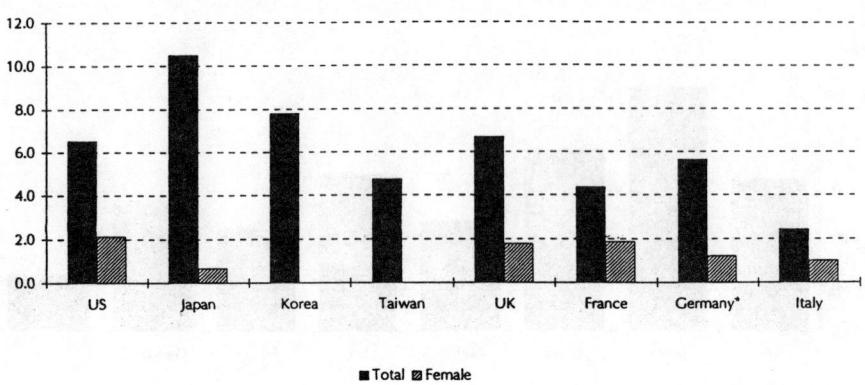

■ Total ▨ Female

ment in research and development, research scientists and engineers (RSEs) as a proxy indicator.

The United States leads the world in its overall employment of RSEs, about 1 million, but Japan has a slightly higher density on a per capita basis, with Europe lagging well behind. Within Europe the UK lags behind France and Germany, while it is ahead of Korea (Figure 4.4). These figures for the UK disguise, however, the fact that in terms of change the employment of RSEs has been growing dramatically in Korea and Taiwan, while the UK growth rate lags

Figure 4.4 RSE per 1,000 labour force

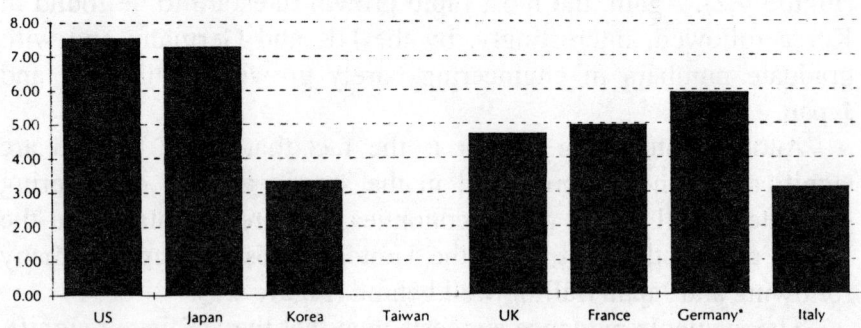

Figure 4.5 Per cent growth in RSE numbers 1985 to 1989

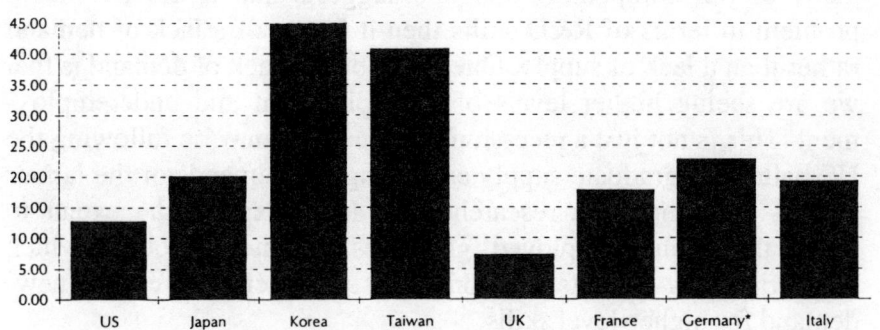

behind even the much lower growth rates of the developed economies of the US, Japan and the major European economies (Figure 4.5). However, in the early years of the 1990s many of these growth rates have gone into reverse in the western economies as a result of the recession. The figures for the UK are made worse by the fact that in the UK a very high proportion of R&D expenditure has been on defence-related activities, where the commercial spin-offs have been lower and there has been little transferability of skills with the private sector, and where investment has been falling fast over and above the recessionary effect.

Thus it can be seen that the 'follower' nations of the Pacific, such as Korea and Taiwan, will soon have pools of HRST equal to the more developed economies. When this data is combined with that relating to scientific activity, for example investment, patents and publications, it can be seen that the major trading blocs, North America, western Europe, Japan and the Pacific Rim countries, are converging in terms of the R&D intensity of their economies. By way of contrast, the R&D intensity of the eastern European states has been falling rapidly with many of their HRST becoming unemployed.

Conclusions
So what do we conclude for the UK? First, the supply of HRST in the UK matches and in some cases exceeds the figures for many of

our competitors and has continued to boom in the UK into the 1990s. Our employment of RSEs, however, lags behind that of many of our competitors and this suggests that if the UK has a problem in terms of R&D skills then it is one of a lack of demand rather than a lack of supply. One result of this lack of demand is that we are seeing higher levels of unemployment and underemployment. This is not just a recessionary effect: we may be following the US pattern of graduate supply exceeding the demands of the labour market. An important research issue is to explore the extent to which these 'underemployed' graduates are entering jobs to which they bring new insights and add value and in effect create a 'new' demand for higher-level skills.

Thus the UK has a strong and still expanding S&T skills base which is not always fully utilised. This comparative advantage is, however, being eroded as the Pacific countries and the 'follower' nations catch up. The key challenge is how we strengthen, rebuild or replace this comparative advantage to ensure competitiveness in the future in an increasingly competitive global marketplace. Further expanding the supply would appear to offer little solution in the absence of a means of enhancing demand.

References

Court G et al. (1994a and annual) *The IES Graduate Review*. Brighton: Institute for Employment Studies

Court G et al. (1994b) *The Labour Market for Graduates in the United States*. Brighton: Institute for Employment Studies

Court G et al. (1994c) 'Non National Recruitment in European Research Centres: Trends and Influences', Report on SPSG Research Programme. Brighton: Institute for Employment Studies

EC (1994) *European Report on Science and Technology Indicators*. Brussels: European Commission

Institute for Employment Research (1994) *Review of the Economy and Employment*. Warwick University

Pearson R and N Jagger (1994) *HRST Working paper for EC* (1994 below). Brighton: Institute for Employment Studies

Pearson R et al. (1989) *How Many Graduates Do We Need in the 21st Century?* Brighton: Institute for Employment Studies (then called IMS)

Pearson R (1994) Manual on the Measurement of Human Resources Devoted to Science Technology 'Canberra manual'. Paris: OECD

Porter M (1990) *The Competitive Advantage of Nations*. London: Macmillan

Weiner M J (1981) *English Culture and the Decline of the Industrial Spirit 1850-1950*. Cambridge: Cambridge University Press

Woods A (1994) *North-South Trade, Employment and Inequality: Changing Fortunes in a Skill-Driven World*. Oxford: Clarendon Press

5 The future of low-skilled jobs

Ken Ducatel

It would be too easy to assume that only high-level professional workers will be needed in the future. This appearance is fuelled both by the increased use of technologies in all areas of industry, and by 'qualification inflation' – many firms now recruit graduates for all career track positions. The appearance, however, belies the reality. Although it is true that many of the jobs created in the boom of the 1980s were professionalised, there were also many jobs created in basic and lower skill grades. Compared to professionalised roles, these jobs are relatively under-researched, perhaps because they are less glamorous and therefore of less appeal to policy-makers. Indeed, the growth of lower-skilled work is often seen as indicative of the development of a low-skill, low-pay sector, typified by downmarket, temporary 'burger flipping' jobs, which require few skills and offer little long-term stability.

To some extent these visions do reflect the emerging picture of a polarising workforce with intellectualised work on the one hand and more routine work on the other. However, this is a rather simplistic picture, which implies that the new, lower-skill work currently being created has little intrinsic merit, creates a tier of workers who are instantly replaceable and contributes to the fragmentation of society. This chapter claims that this is only a partial view, implying, moreover, that there is a realistic alternative to the creation of large numbers of relatively low-skilled jobs. In practical policy terms, these jobs are necessary to provide work for a large number of workers (and potential workers) currently in and about to enter the labour market. The challenge is not to create high-skill employment for all, that would be impossible, but to create lower-skill occupations which provide longer-term economic opportunities, which can reliably satisfy people's work, social and lifestyle aspirations.

The growth of low-skilled work in the UK

The jobs growth which occurred in the 1980s in the UK had five key features: it was service sector-led; it was driven (in part) by processes of externalisation or sub-contracting; most of the job creation was for part-time employees; most of the growth in the labour market was among women; and there was, in the UK at least, a significant rise in self-employment.

First, most of the growth has occurred in the service sector, although there has been some growth in information technology-intensive manufacturing industries. The service sector is notoriously hard to define (see the discussion in Ducatel and Miles, 1995). One way to think about services is in terms of the types of market which the services serve and the way in which they are delivered (Table 5.1). State services have undergone a massive expansion since the middle of the twentieth century, accounting for a large share of job generation. Their future growth is in dispute through the rise of neo-liberalism and the associated programmes of privatisation and the creation of quasi-markets. Consumer services have traditionally been provided locally because they have usually required the consumer and provider to be co-located (in the same place at the same time). There is a trend towards the separation of delivery and consumption, through standardisation of services and automation. However, this trend is held in check by the uneasy compromise between increased customisation and standardisation of customer services. Producer services were the great growth trend of the 1980s, with many new specialist services being sought out by businesses in response to increased market volatility, heightened competition and rapid technological change. Of course there are also 'mixed' services which represent a blend of each of the market types.

Second, the growth in producer services has been fuelled by increased sub-contracting within industry as well as an expansion of the service sector per se. That is, many jobs have been reclassified into the service sector, because they are no longer done in-house but are provided by specialist service sector firms. Externalised services tend to be either:

Future skill demand and supply

Table 5.1
A two-dimensional classification of services

Market type	Production type		
	Physical service	Person centred	Informational
State		Welfare Hospital Health Medical Education	Public administration Broadcasting
Consumer	Domestic service Catering Retail trade Post	Barbers Hairdressers	Entertainment
Mixed	Laundries Hotels Repairs Telecoms Banking Insurance Legal services		Real estate
Producer	Wholesale trade Freight transport & storage		Engineering & architectural Accountancy Miscellaneous professional

Source: Ducatel and Miles, 1995

- high-skill complex services, such as advertising, facilities management, computer software, accountancy and legal services;
- lower-skill services such as catering, cleaning and security.

Third, many of the jobs which have been created in the last decade have been part-time. In overall terms, the number of full-time jobs in the economy has stagnated while part-timers have grown by 20 per cent to represent 25 per cent of the workforce

Table 5.2
Hours actually worked (per person per year)

	1970	1983	1992
France	1962	1711	1666
Norway	1766	1471	1417
Sweden	1641	1453	1485
United States	1886	1788	1769

Source: Freeman and Soete, 1994

(*Economist*, 12 March 1994). Thus, although there are now more jobs in the economy, the volume of labour which is absorbed is not necessarily as large because of a secular trend in most countries towards declining annual working time (unfortunately, unlike some other countries, data on labour volume is not consistently recorded for the UK – see Table 5.2).

Fourth, most of the new labour market entrants are female. Over the long term a redistribution of work has taken place, with female activity rates rising steadily since the 1950s. Women now represent nearly 50 per cent of the workforce in the UK, but they are still

Table 5.3
Women's share of jobs in the EU (1980s)

Females as per cent of occupational group	
Personal, catering and security	66
Clerical	64
Sales and managers	49
Professional and technical	45
Agricultural	34
Government admin and managerial	23
Production, transport and construction	16

Source: Rubery and Fagan, 1994 (based on European Community Labour Force Survey: EC 11, excluding Italy).

heavily concentrated in the lower-skilled occupations and in part-time work. In 1991, women made up 90 per cent of the part-time workforce, but only about 35 per cent of the full-time workforce and one quarter of the self employed (Meager and Williams, 1994).

Fifth, there was a large expansion of self-employment in the UK during the 1980s, a large body of which was in relatively low-skilled and marginal occupations and trades. Across Europe this growth in self-employment is unique, with many countries showing stagnant or declining self-employment trends (Table 5.4). (The only other countries which showed significant growth in self-employment were Ireland and the Netherlands, and this was an increase of around a quarter, not the near doubling which took place in the UK.)

Table 5.4
Self-employment trends (index : 1975=100)

	1973	1981	1984	1989
UK	104.1	111.4	139.3	182.5
Denmark	no data	89.7	80.1	77.6
France	102.9	96.8	99.8	97.3
Germany	104.0	95.5	101.3	104.4
Netherlands	106.0	110.2	96.9*	124.5

* Data for 1985
Source: Meager et al., 1994

Low-skill occupations

These five key trends reflect some of the main dimensions of current and, most probably, future growth in employment in the UK. If we focus down on occupational changes in the UK, there are some consistent trends across a wide variety of industries, which indicate a need to take the future of lower-skilled work much more seriously than has been the case historically. The first thing to note is that direct production work, which still accounts for the vast bulk of job categories in the standard classification of occupations, has shown a continuing tendency to decline in absolute and relative terms (Figure 5.1). The implication is that overall the economy might be expected to contain fewer and fewer full-time manual jobs (skilled and un-

Table 5.5
The growth of lower-skilled work in Ireland 1971-1996

Thousands

Occupation	1971	1990	1996	% Female 1990
Drivers	29.8	35.9	36.5	3.7
Other security workers	6.2	13.4	16.8	8.5
Sales agents	13.3	20.9	22.7	16.8
Sales assistants	52.2	56.6	63.0	50.9
Catering	11.4	13.7	18.5	69.9
Other personal service work	45.8	47.9	58.7	72.2
Typists	23.1	34.4	38.8	95.7
Clerks	82.5	104.3	110.9	68.9

Source: Corocan et al., 1993

skilled) – and we had better start thinking about how we can deal with that trend. It has direct implications for the structure of basic education and training schemes, and even for the culture of work in the country.

By the same token, if current trends continue, we may not be able to look to some traditional areas of white-collar employment, such as clerical work, to create enough new jobs in growing industries to compensate for the decline in manufacturing industries (Figure 5.2). Instead, the emerging employment among lower-skill workers has predominantly fallen into the category we might call sales, security, cleaning and catering (Figure 5.3). This growth has been largest in the 'Social and human services' and the 'Material and physical services' (Figures 5.4 and 5.5). (By contrast the other growth areas of 'Informational services' and 'Assembly and variable manufacturing' have mostly created jobs for professional and managerial occupational groups, Figures 5.6 and 5.7).

Figures which show occupational growth for Ireland over the past 20 years indicate the scale of growth which has occurred in some lower-skill occupations, which, although in Ireland, are likely to be comparable to the UK (Table 5.5). It is worth noting that the growing occupation sectors are mostly either dominantly male or

Future skill demand and supply

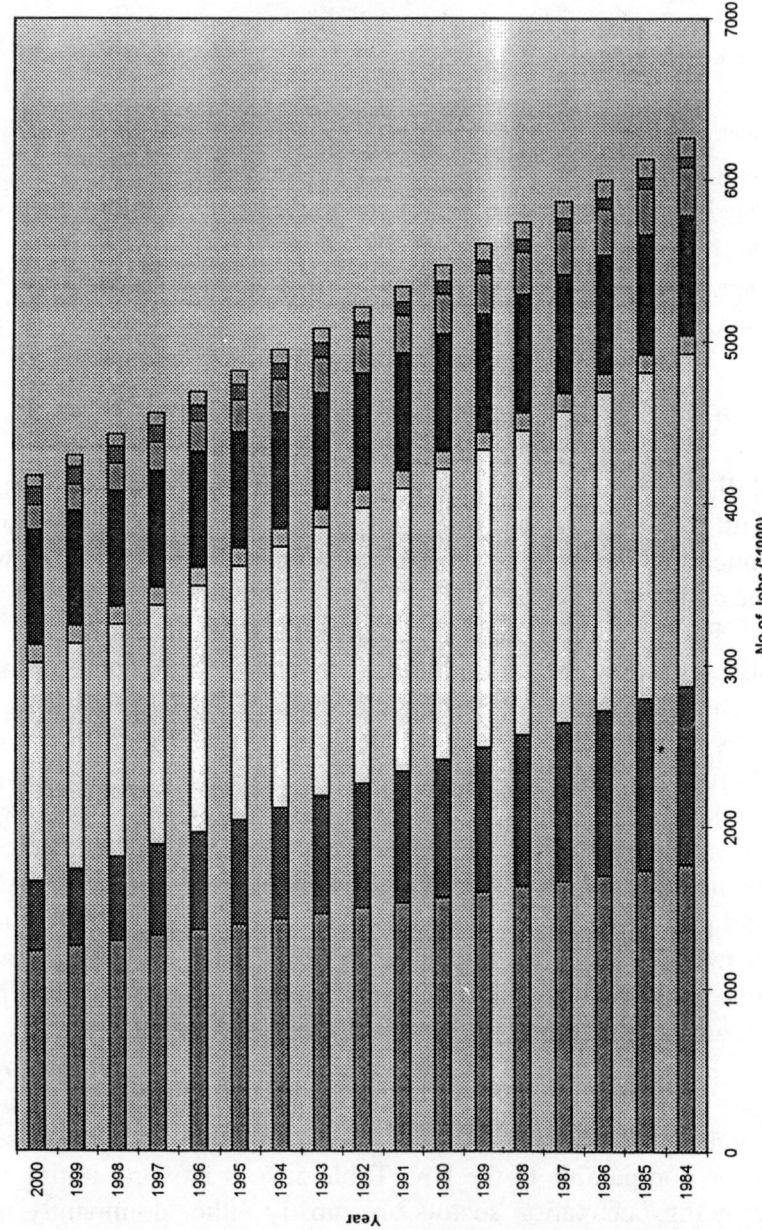

Figure 5.1 Predicted employment for workers in the production field, all companies

The future of low-skilled jobs

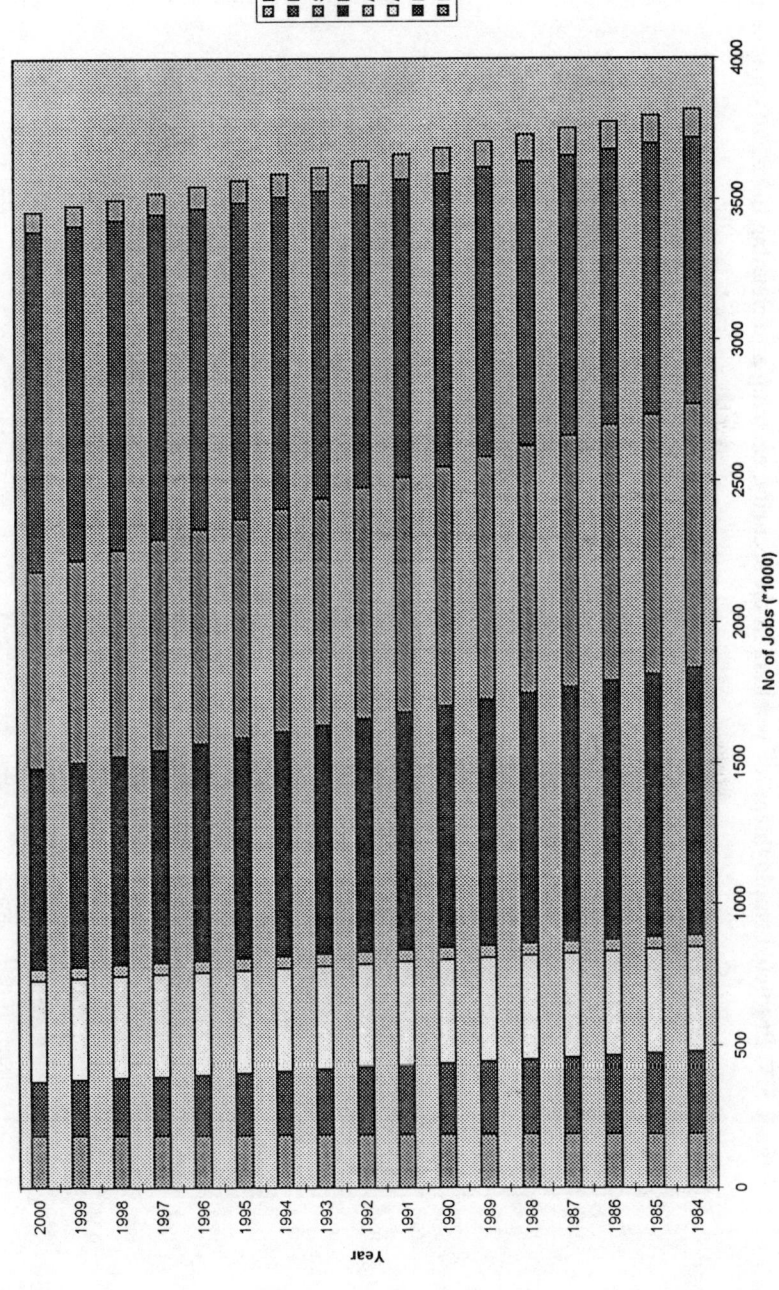

Figure 5.2 Predicted employment for workers in the clerical field, all companies

Figure 5.3 Predicted employment for workers in the security, catering and cleaning fields, all companies

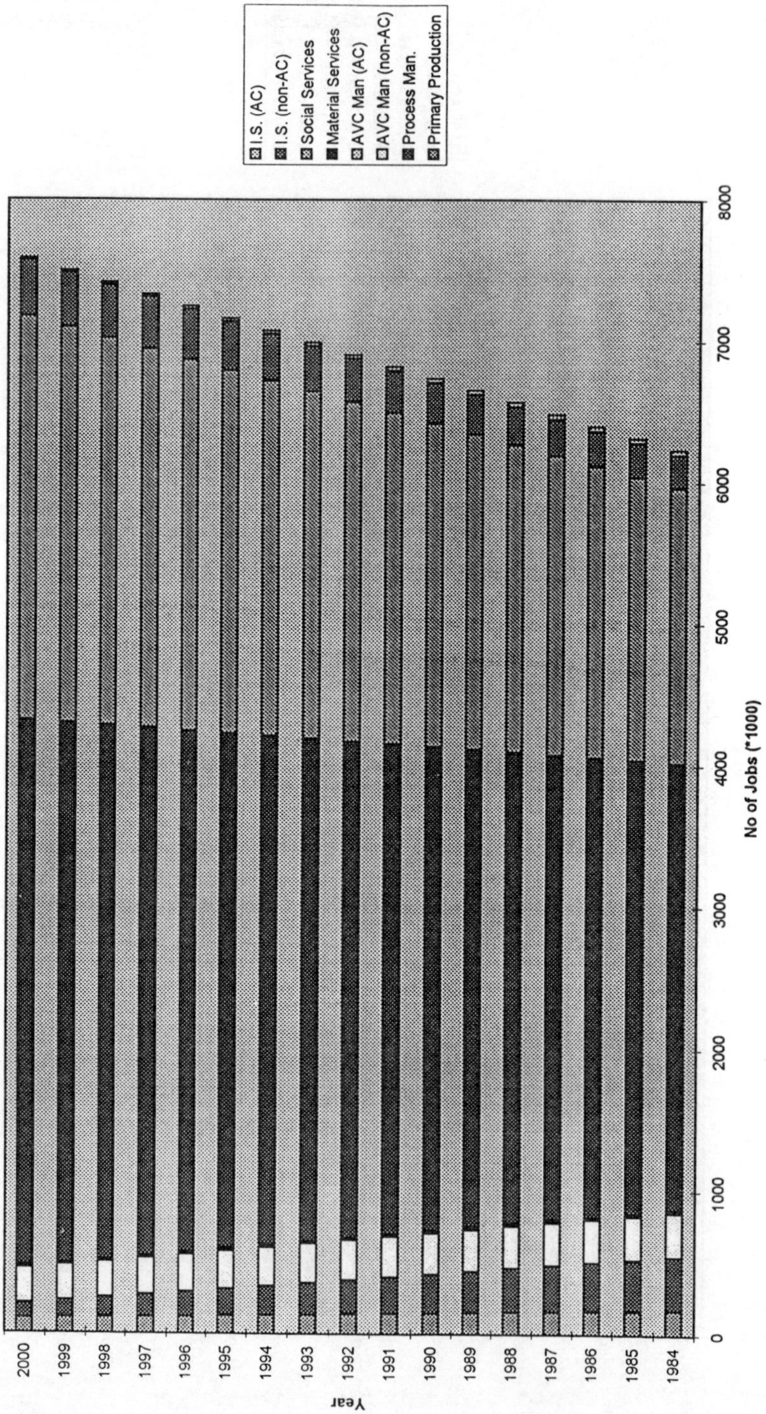

The future of low-skilled jobs

Figure 5.4 Predicted percentage distribution of jobs in the social and human services industry, all companies

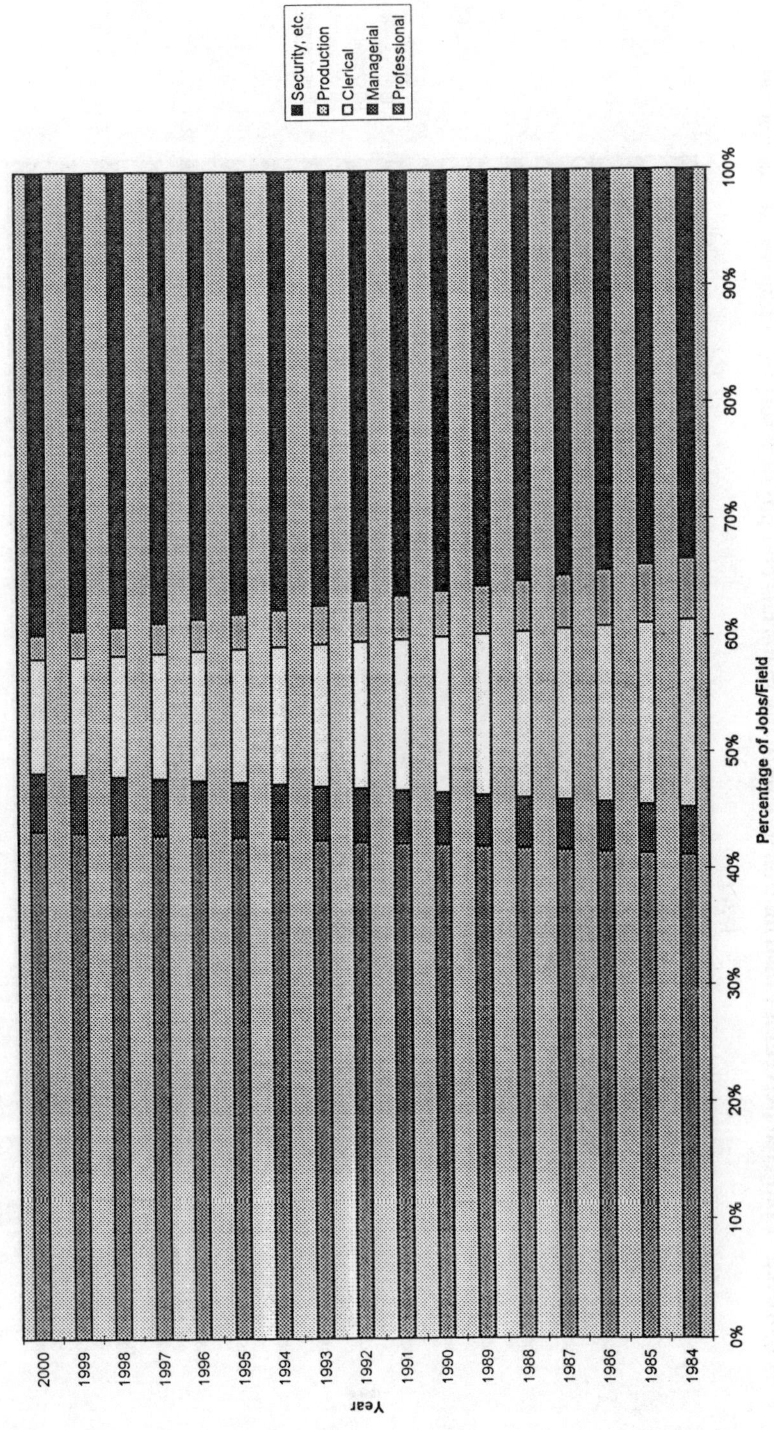

Future skill demand and supply

Figure 5.5 Predicted percentage distribution of jobs in the materials and physical services industry, all companies

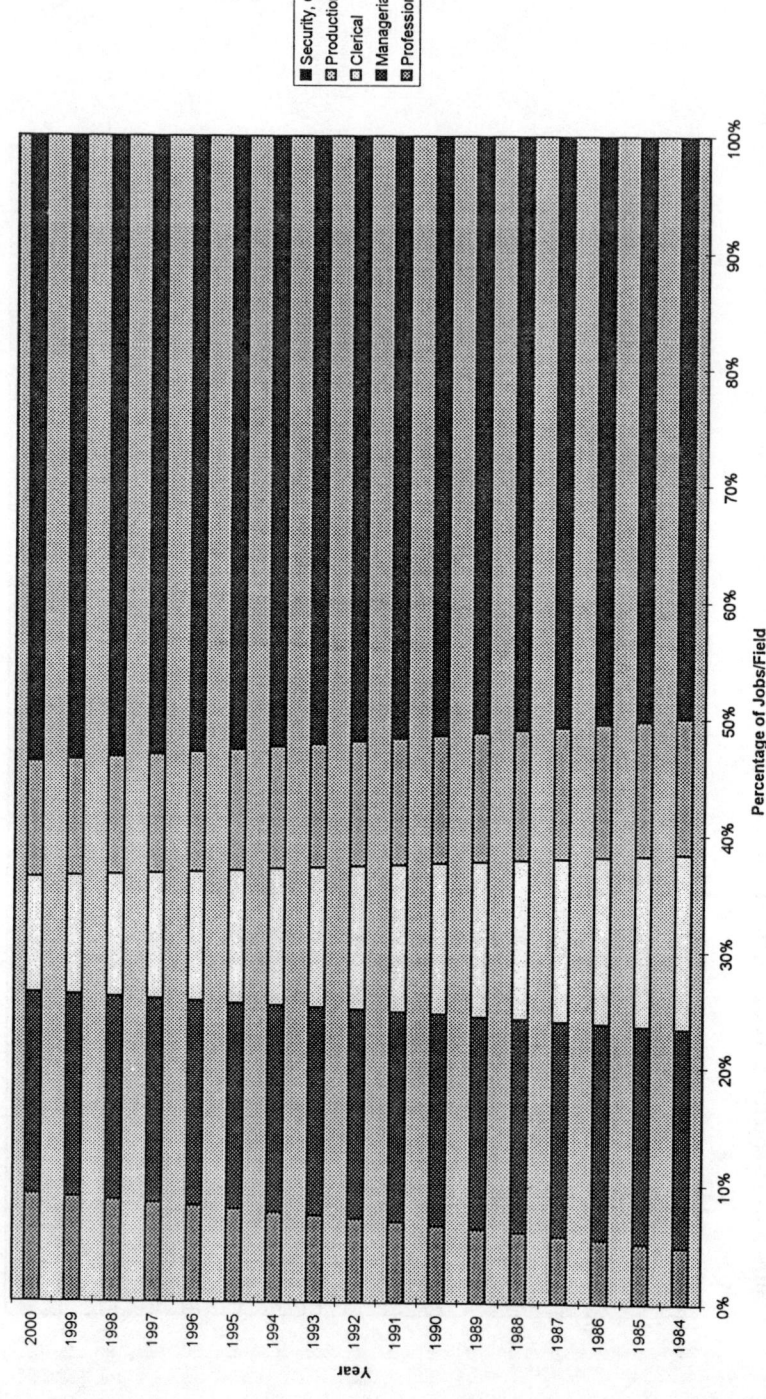

The future of low-skilled jobs

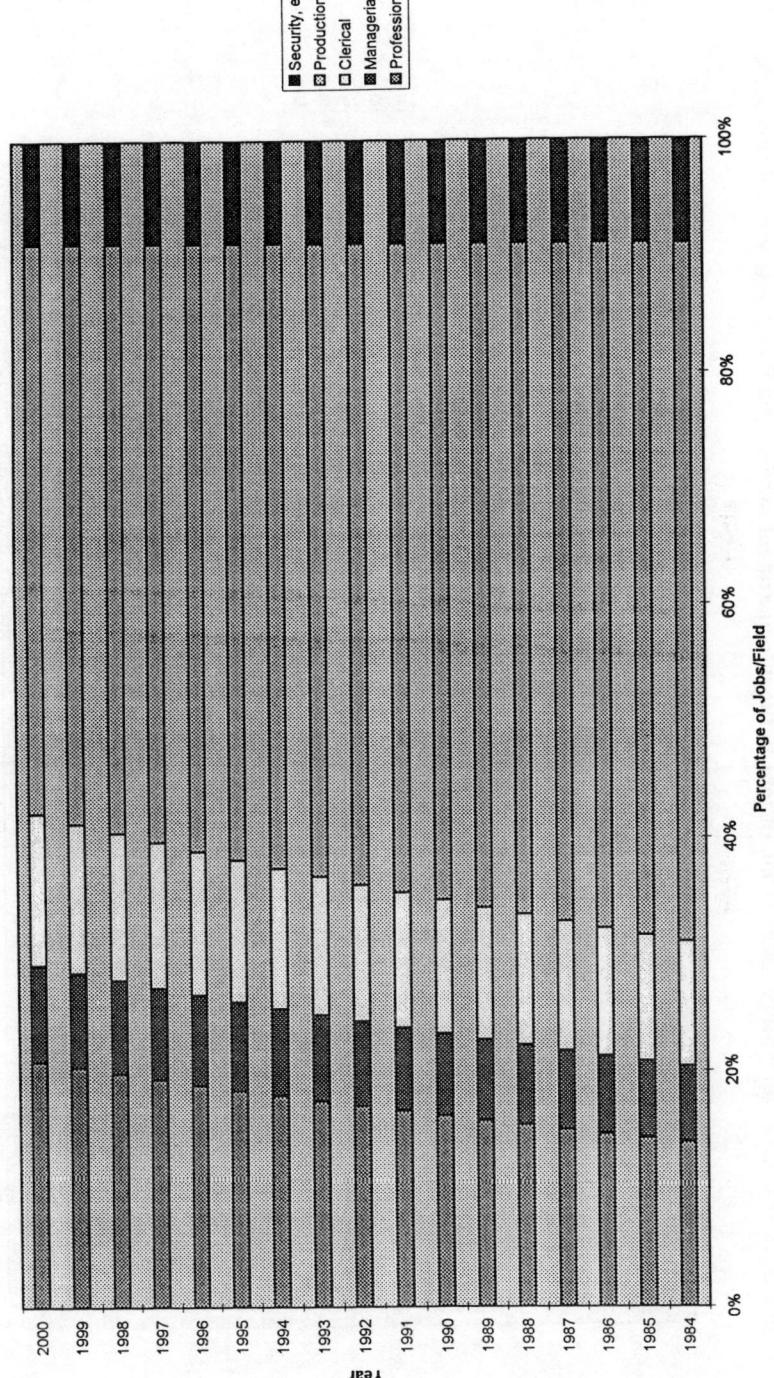

Figure 5.6 Predicted percentage distribution of jobs in the AVC manufacturing (non-AC) industry, all companies

67

Future skill demand and supply

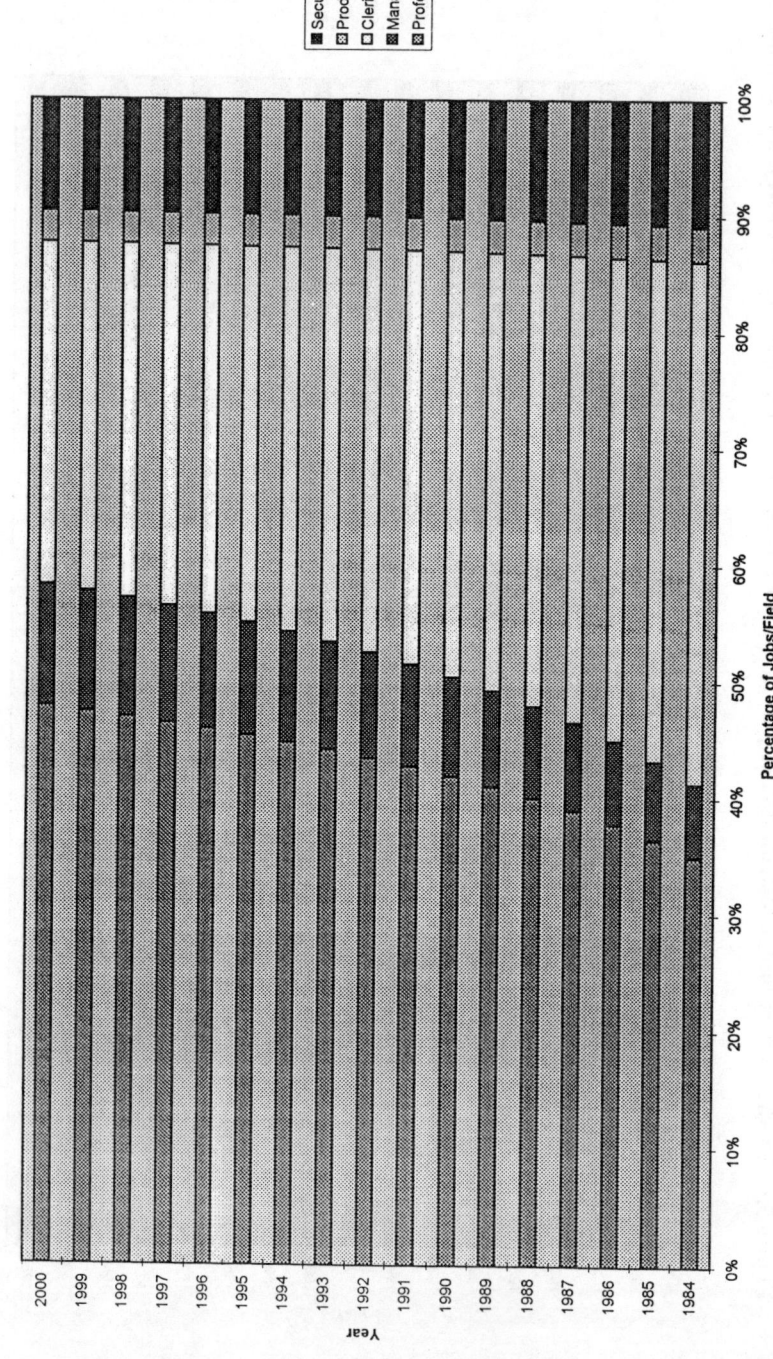

Figure 5.7 Predicted percentage distribution of jobs in the informational services (non-AC) industry, all companies

68

dominantly female, with only sales occupations showing a more even split. Generally, in the UK female participation is higher, but it has also been rising steadily across all occupations in Ireland over the past 20 years.

The low-skill/low-wage/low-hope economy?

Clearly, therefore, there is significant growth in lower-skilled work in certain sectors, which is important in terms of generating economic opportunities for the wide range of people who are unlikely to become highly educated professionals or even to acquire the status of skilled manual workers. The persistent high level of unemployment in the economy, however, makes it obvious that, despite the increased flexibility of labour markets in the UK, there are still insufficient jobs to go around. Thus, one aspect of policy has to concern itself with the rate at which lower-skilled jobs can be created. But, beyond the sheer number of jobs, there are serious concerns about whether the job opportunities for people with lower skills provide a satisfying work experience or are adequate to sustain family life. The answers to these questions are mixed and again should provoke a policy response.

The issue of the number of jobs created is particularly hard to untangle, as the UK faces a skills mismatch between the capabilities of the people in the labour market and the opportunities available. This is not a simple structural problem due to the rapid change in the technological base, with too few technically qualified personnel, such as programmers and systems analysts, and too many traditionally skilled people, such as those with traditional craft skills, electromechanical know-how and so on. The skills gap also includes cultural and social aspects of work, even in the service sector. The management interest in 'total quality management', 'employee empowerment' or 'customer service programmes', during the 1980s, underlines the need (however inadequately realised) for workers to be more involved or incorporated in the objectives of the firm or organisation.

Quality or customer service programmes have been implemented all the way down the organisational hierarchy. It is especially important in service sector organisations that they be adopted by the personnel directly engaged in delivering services to end users (as firms or as direct personal consumers). As already mentioned, this creates a contradiction for many, labour-intensive, service organisations: on the one hand, service quality is increasingly seen as a competitive weapon, on the other hand there is a temptation to squeeze the payroll either by hiring cheaper workers or by replacing workers wherever possible by standardising or automating services. It is hard to achieve both aims at the same time. The result is too often the false, or forced, obsequiousness of service personnel: that results in the cringe-inducing 'Have a nice day'. Clearly, workers are under considerable pressure, for fear of losing their deregulated and flexibilised jobs, to provide a higher level of service than would have been acceptable in the past. Nevertheless, it is hard for really alienated workers to maintain a convincing facade of friendliness (or customer service orientation), without a fundamental shift in organisational culture. This shift seems to be strongly under way or to have taken place in many consumer service organisations, at least so far as front of house operations are concerned. Thus, recruitment in these 'lower-skilled' occupations would seem to centre strongly on the personal attributes of individuals, their ability to communicate effectively and coherently and to have a reasonable knowledge of the organisation and its products and services.

The shift towards customer awareness raises new questions about our understanding of 'skill' – which has ever been a definitional minefield. One of the clearest examples of new forms of skill, based upon the possession of desirable social aptitudes, can be found in the, now well known, work of Applebaum and Albin (1989). In a study of the effect of new technology on clerical skills in the general insurance industry they noted two broad organisational responses to information technology, which they called the algorithmic and robust organisational forms. The algorithmic organisation basically used information technology to reinforce a bureaucratic division of labour, with a rigid division of labour between field sales personnel, back office data entry workers and workers engaged in the various stages of automated form feeding, insurance policy issuing and dealing with claims. The robust organisational form represented a significant move forward in the application of IT in the workplace. Here, many of the routine tasks were replaced by a group of customer sales or claim representatives, supported by an on-line policy and claim system, who were able to resolve the entire range of straightforward issues which a customer might encounter. This required a wider individual knowledge of insurance policy issuing and claim procedures. In turn each representative had to have a greater degree of skill. However, the levels of skill involved were relatively easily learnt during a five-week classroom training course, followed by three to five months on the job experience. Moreover, the extra productivity of the staff allowed the firm to increase sales whilst reducing staff. The example of the shift towards robust organisations indicates in some detail the new types of skill which are being demanded of even lesser-skilled individuals – personality attributes, the ability to communicate effectively, the knowledge of products and services (which are likely to be continually changing), basic computer literacy, and most of all flexibility and the willingness to learn and adapt.

At first sight, the quality of work would seem to be on an upward trend, but the robust organisation, described by Applebaum and Albin, had its downsides. First, the on-line technology allowed the direct surveillance of personnel who were constantly aware that they were subject to scrutiny through performance targets and by supervisors directly listening in. The result of such systems is a potential increase in stress levels – depending on how managers implement the surveillance systems. Such surveillance technologies are not limited to telephone-based sales operations, but include any networked technology such as bar code readers at the retail checkout or mobile communications systems in the driver's cab.

Second, the general interest level of the work may have increased and also the skills demanded may have moved upwards, but the workers concerned received no extra financial rewards for their extra skill and commitment. The company concerned had struck a win-win deal, in that its payroll costs had fallen and productivity had risen simultaneously. In traditional unionised workplaces one of the standard bargaining issues on the introduction of new technology has always been extra payment for learning extra skills, there was none of that here.

Third, the new on-line systems are often operated over a longer working day than has been traditional. For instance, the new wave of electronic back offices which provide telephone support to customers, often called 'Call Centres', frequently stay open to 9 or 10pm. This has encouraged the shift towards part-time working, with an optimum shift period before the worker becomes stale, estimated at around four hours (Richardson, 1994). The attraction of part-time workers, therefore, is not merely that they have historically been cheaper and less protected than full-time workers, but also that they can be used to support the move towards longer operating hours, spread over a seven-day week.

One big question mark over the future of lower-skilled employment, therefore, is less about its position numerically, but more about its viability for the workers concerned. In the absence of bargaining power (with continuing high levels of unemployment and job insecurity) the danger is that the wages of such workers will be driven down to uneconomic levels. This is exacerbated by the fact that a large share of the growth in part-time employment is marginal employment. Two key areas of employment growth illustrate how marginal employment might drive out real long-term job opportunities. It has been suggested, by the Institute of Fiscal Studies, that low-paid part-timers are often the wives of working husbands or are young people living at home (cited in the *Economist* 16 April 1994). For instance, the classic picture of a US back office worker is a middle-class housewife willing to work for lower wages as long as the hours and the location are convenient (Nelson, 1986). Second, many of the 'burger flipping' jobs are taken by young people who are in a temporary limbo in the labour market, or who are still studying full or part-time. This is well illustrated in the case of McDonalds which has grown over the past 20 years to 550 outlets in the UK. Only nine per cent of its 32,000 employees are over 32, and the vast majority (88 per cent) work fewer than 35 hours per week for an average of £128.80 in Central London, or less elsewhere (*The Guardian,* 1 October 1994). By contrast, the really poor are relatively less likely to work at all. In families with dependent children, where the husband is out of work, only one per cent of wives work, and fewer than 50 per cent of lone mothers are in work.

The pattern of low pay for low-skill work, therefore, is not straightforwardly linked to the emergence of an employed underclass. The subtext is that young people will go on from McDonalds to more stable higher-paid employment, and that the wives are not trapped in irksome job roles, because the household does not vitally depend on their income. Of course, neither of these two conditions may hold in reality. For instance, there is still a significant worry that younger workers will not make the transition into regular em-

Table 5.6
Job growth industries in the US

Industry	Total employees (thousands)		Average hourly wage of production workers (US$)	
	1980	1990	1980	1990
Computer and DP services	304	704	7.16	15.10
Legal services	498	919	7.35	14.21
Advertising	153	238	8.07	13.52
Hospitals	2,750	3,547	6.06	11.79
Utilities	829	961	8.90	15.24
Trucking and warehousing	1,280	1,638	9.13	11.72
Wholesale trade	5,292	6,205	6.95	10.79
Nursing & personal care	997	1,420	4.17	7.25
Beauty shops	284	373	4.26	7.10
Hotels and motels	1,038	1,595	4.45	6.99
Retail trade	15,018	19,683	4.88	6.76
Eating and drinking places	4,626	6,565	3.69	4.97

Source: Derived from US Bureau of Statistics, quoted in Freeman and Soete, 1994

ployment. As has happened elsewhere in Europe (especially Spain and Italy), there is a large-scale labour market 'underclass' of workers who are effectively excluded from 'normal life-cycle patterns', because of their inability to establish a permanent and self-sustaining position in the labour market. That is to say that they often have to defer starting families, establishing permanent homes away from the family home and so on. (See Mingione, 1991, for an excellent discussion of the wider social implications of these problems.)

Using recent US data as indicative (although in the US more of the new jobs which have been created in the 1980s are full-time positions), it is possible to see that there is vast variation in the wage scales of the jobs being created in lower-skill occupations (Table 5.6). The hourly rates for production workers in the professionalised services sector are up to three times the rates for lower-skilled workers in the restaurant trade. By the same token, production workers in the male dominated transport and utilities industries are between twice and three times those in the hospitality services and retail trade. These variations are more accentuated in the US case than in Europe; nevertheless, the general pattern of divergence is roughly similar, especially in Britain. Figures from the Department of Employment indicate a general range of gross pay for skilled occupations of between £3.20 (for female bar staff and hairdressers) to just short of £5.00 (for male receptionists and security guards). The general picture is that women's wages tend to lag behind in these jobs – although, interestingly, female security guards seem to make considerably more than their male counterparts.

The point is that a mix of factors lies behind these pay variations, including: issues of gendered work roles, permanent or temporary employment systems, full or part-time employment and most probably rates of unionisation in the case of the male dominated production workers. The key question is whether the lower-skilled work being created in these service sectors actually represents a long-term option for a self-supporting lifestyle, or is it a long-term low-wage trap from which escape can only be made through high qualifications and skills. Moreover, as long as the middle ground between professionalised roles and lower-skilled roles continues to disappear, the chances of gaining promotion from a lower-skilled job inevitably become lower and lower.

A new entrepreneurial spirit?

If jobs are not available or are unviable, then perhaps one way to create them would be for the people concerned to take the initiative themselves by setting up their own firms or by working in the informal sector. Taking the latter idea first, the prospect of a growing informal sector certainly did not dismay Margaret Thatcher, in her celebrated comment on it providing evidence of an emerging entrepreneurial culture. However, there are perhaps stronger links between the marginally employed and the growing informal economy, with people who are unable to establish a permanent presence in the labour market resorting to illicit activities in order to survive. There does indeed seem to be a rough correlation between high rates of unemployment and the size of the informal economy (Table 5.7). However, as the work of both Mingione (1991) and Pahl (1988) has indicated, the informal economy is often strongest amongst people

Table 5.7
Unemployment and the informal economy

	Unemployment as % of labour force (1993)	The informal economy as % of GDP
Spain	23	25
Italy	12	21
Belgium	10	14
Sweden	8	14
Germany	9	9
France	12	8
Britain	10	7
US	6	7
Holland	7	7
Japan	3	4
Switzerland	5	4

Source: *Economist,* 12 February 1994

who are already in employment. Their findings were that informal work is used as a supplement to existing regular employment, such as auto mechanics moonlighting by repairing neighbours' cars or teachers providing individual tuition. Indeed, it seems that the people on the very lowest rungs of the employment ladder (or those that have fallen off it altogether) are those who have most trouble gaining access to any forms of employment. Just as with lower-paid employment, the informal sector is hard to access for people who are amongst the very poor.

By contrast, self-employment and small businesses have been sold as a major engine of economic revitalisation throughout the 1980s and into the 1990s. As we have already seen, the growth in self-employment in the UK in the 1980s was remarkable in comparison with other European countries. However, this boom in self-employment is related to a mix of drivers, not all of which are due to a rising tide of entrepreneurialism and enthusiasm for the free market (Meager et al, 1994):

1. Rising unemployment may have pushed people into involuntary self-employment through the absence of alternatives and, possibly, the availability of a relatively large (on the basis of personal experience) redundancy payment. However, as Meager (1992) points out, self-employment during a recessional phase is less likely to result in a viable business than growth phase start-ups.

2. The trend towards a service economy tips the balance in favour of self-employment, as service firms are overall more likely to operate as small firms or sole traders.

3. The processes of externalisation and contracting out have also propelled many people into self-employment. In short, if they wish to carry on doing the same job, workers increasingly have to hire themselves out as freelance or labour only workers. There is some dispute about the scale of this trend, and whether it is simply a means for employers to externalise some of the costs of employment, or whether the growth of small producer service firms represents a viable form of employment for a large number of workers.

The setting up of a small business in order to escape or avoid unemployment seems much more common in the UK than elsewhere in Europe. (Table 5.8). However, there is considerable doubt whether workers who are starting a small business from a position of unemployment or labour market inactivity are likely to generate a

Table 5.8
From unemployment to self employment in Europe

	Inflows to self-employment from unemployment (%)		
	1982-3	1984-5	1988-9
UK	2.5	3.3	5.2
Greece	4.0	2.9	2.3
France	1.5	1.7	1.9
Belgium	1.4	1.4	1.4
Germany	1.2	0.7	0.8

Source: Meager et al, 1994

self-sustaining business. Notwithstanding the 100,000 or so firm starts which were generated each year during the bulk of the 1980s under the 'Enterprise Allowance' scheme, unemployed people are much more likely to occupy the lowest position on the income scale. The growth of personal, catering and cleaning services, which is in part reflected in this band of female, part-time self-employment, forms a particularly worrying trend towards forms of self-employment which are based upon self-exploitation. Of particular concern where jobs are hard to come by, is that as fresh waves of lower-skill workers set themselves up as self employed, the price they can charge for their services is driven down to a level which is sub-economic.

Labour policy and lower-skilled employment
The purpose of this paper has been to re-examine some of the issues which surround the future of lower-skilled employment. One of the intentions has been to provide a counterbalance to the notion that in the future there will only be a demand for high-skilled professional workers. Under all reasonable expectations, one can expect a wide range of employment opportunities to be generated for non-graduate level employees. However, the content required of lower-skilled work is shifting and there is a basis for concern that these jobs form a long-term low-wage trap for those that take them up.

As regards the content of the work, there is a clear shift in emphasis of skills, even at the lower level. Low levels of literacy, unwillingness to use or total ignorance of computer systems, poor communication skills and the inability to respond to a changing work environment will be the major barriers to getting work in even the most lowly positions in the future. This is of major concern because there is evidence to suggest that there may be as many as six million adults in the UK who experience basic numeracy, reading and writing difficulties (Holmes, 1989). (The number with severe difficulties is lower; nevertheless the estimates indicate that around 600,000 are illiterate, that is unable to read or write at all, with many more unable to do simple sums.) As Meager and Williams (1994) note, even if very low-skilled people manage to enter the labour market, they are unlikely to climb up a career ladder, because 'the additional importance of basic skills for promotion, over and above their importance for actually doing the job, is most marked in the least skilled jobs, where there are generally fewer opportunities for internal progression' (p.62). Moreover, workplace learning for people with lower than basic skills tends to be very unevenly provided, and is highly focused on meeting the specific work role needs, without much attention to wider learning experiences (Atkinson, 1992).

The concept of 'basic' or lower skill levels is clearly dynamic. As general skill levels rise, or as some technologies become pervasive, such as the automobile or the computers, then the minimum threshold for entering and maintaining employment also tends to go up. However, across a wide range of skill levels, future employability seems to be shifting towards tacit skills, which may sometimes require quite a high level of personal ability, even if these abilities are not directly rewarded in financial terms. Thus, this chapter has concentrated upon the growing demand for communication skills, the ability to respond to change, to work co-operatively and a willingness to take responsibility. This shift in skills does not per se seem to lead to better working conditions for employees. Rather, in many cases while the job may be more interesting than say a routine clerical or manual job, there seems to be an increased level of stress, pace of work and uncertainty about the stability of employment.

Although tacit skills seem to be growing in importance, they seem to retain some of the key features with which they have been associated. First, tacit skills tend to be under-rewarded, as the costs of obtaining them are socialised. Second, many tacit skills such as the ability to communicate, to work with others and to be personable are ones which are associated with support workers, such as secretaries, receptionists, sales assistants and so on. These jobs tend also to be under-rewarded, in this case because they are predominantly filled by women. Third, tacit skills are still too often regarded as personal characteristics rather than ones which can be taught or learnt. Thus, people are recruited on the basis of personality. This creates a double inefficiency. People with more formal skills avoid these roles because they are not associated with a career path. People in these roles find it hard to demonstrate that they have the competence to move up the career ladder. One wonders whether the old indictment about job enrichment 'I don't feel enriched just knackered'

(Nichols and Beynon, 1977), might be replaced with 'How can you be empowered on £3.68 an hour?'.

A key problem for many people with lower skill levels may not be so much that they lack the skills necessary to compete in the labour market, but the skills which are needed are regarded as generally available or at least not certificated. The tendency for most career track occupations to require paper qualifications at entry, and for these to be continuously updated throughout a working life, creates a strong two-tiered structure to the labour market. These sorts of barriers to upward mobility are nothing new, however, they have long been observed in respect to women's work, where it is very hard for women to gain access to and then move up in male dominated technical and professional occupations (see, for instance, Teresa Rees' discussion of policies to overcome these barriers in Rees, 1994).

More and better training systems is, of course, one of the standard recommendations of the literature on labour market policy. Poor skill levels and training provision have long been associated with poor competitiveness. Cross-national studies, for instance, have indicated that technology may be implemented in a sub-optimal manner not because of managerial incompetence, but because the options for technology management are restricted through poor skills at shopfloor level (Prais and Wagner, 1988). Poor skills are also thought to lead to: poor quality products; poor communication with customers (and thus lost orders); high wastage rates; time wasted fixing mistakes; limited organisational flexibility; and a heavy supervisory burden (Rapp, 1991).

The conclusions here are not going to overturn these well-established conclusions. However, there is a slightly different emphasis here than might be found elsewhere. The first question is whether we can coordinate better the skills demands of employers and the training needs of employees. There is strong evidence to indicate that the structure of local provision of training is inadequate and dislocated, not meeting the needs of employers, employees or the local community. Survey research in South London indicates that many firms have little enthusiasm for government training schemes or Training and Enterprise Councils (TECs). For instance, only 10 per cent of small engineering and business service firms in Croydon made use of training for work programmes and only 20 per cent offered youth training placements (MHA, 1994a). The Croydon example is useful in that a complementary study has been conducted into the problems of unemployment, which included an analysis of the employment and training services in the borough (MHA, 1994b). The conclusions of this report reinforced a general impression that despite the growth of services to tackle unemployment and a poor skills base, the level of resources available was well below what was necessary. Training for employment programmes run by Croydon's continuing education and training service were able to reach 1,300 of the borough's 13,000 unemployed in 1993. The local TEC, SOLOTEC's target figure for achieving job placements and vocational qualifications was 800 per year, against more than 28,000 people in the area experiencing unemployment for more than six months. The general picture was of under-resourced and poorly integrated training provision.

In addition to the general under-provision and poor reflection of local needs, the report added the more damning finding that the structure of training provision effectively excluded many lower-skilled potential trainees from the programmes. For instance, most programmes were concentrated on a narrow band of younger women because selection procedures required prior keyboard experience for an IT course (thus putting off older office workers) and because they concentrated on short-term elementary and introductory courses (mainly at NVQ1 level).

The emerging structure of lower-skilled work, in which it is hard to get off the bottom rung of the job ladder, was compounded in the Croydon case by the absence or retrenchment of adult and continuing training which would allow the employed and the unemployed to progress to higher and more useful qualifications. This area seems to be particularly important. Firms and government training schemes acting together are more likely to produce an upward path for lower-skilled employees which will allow them to develop a range of employment skills which in turn should increase their labour market value by making them more productive.

A second area of conclusions, concerning lower-skilled work, which has relatively recently become very popular following the Delors White Paper, is the idea that there is a wide range of 'social jobs' which are necessary yet are not likely to be provided in the economy. This is the concept of generating a 'sheltered' tradable

Table 5.9
New sources of work

Type of job	Examples
Local services	Home help; child minding; assistance to young people; caretaking of buildings; leisure industry jobs; support of otherwise unviable local services
Quality of life improvements	Renovation of old housing; development of local transport services to meet social and community needs
Environmental protection	Maintenance of natural and public areas; cleaning up polluted areas; monitoring of environmental quality; installing energy-saving equipment

Source: ECSC-EEC-EAEC, 1993

sector of the economy. In the Delors White Paper there is explicit mention of the new jobs in local services, improving the quality of life and environmental protection, and many of these require relatively low skill levels (Table 5.9). In effect, the report argues that such work should be made available on a subsidised basis, where necessary, so that social needs are fulfilled which would not be met through the marketplace, and in order to reduce the economic burden of unemployment. The suggested mechanisms for achieving this are through income tax deductions, special rates of taxation, social employers and service vouchers (which could be used to buy social services).

It is debatable whether the exact examples suggested in the Delors White paper would be acceptable to the UK government, given its focus on market mechanisms and the reduction of public sector spending. A more acceptable approach may be that suggested by Freeman and Soete (1994), in which they develop the idea of using a non-tradable sector in the economy to mop up large numbers of lower skilled employees. The basic concept is derived from the observation that many people are willing to work for lower rates of pay in the informal economy or to engage in self-provision, and thereby virtually discount the cost of their labour. By adjusting tax rates to favour certain non-traded (that is ones which cannot be imported or exported) activities, it is hoped that some of these services might come back into the formal economy and thus contribute to wider employment opportunities in these sectors. As the main areas of predicted high employment growth are in services such as caring and personal services and repair and maintenance, which are prone to being conducted in the informal economy, a system of tax relief for both the provision and purchase of the services could encourage growth in these areas of lower-skilled work.

Overall, the arguments of this chapter have pointed towards the need to take lower-skilled employment more seriously than has generally been the case in the past. First, we need to realise that this employment is not an embarrassing residual category, which exists simply through inadequate industrial and labour market policies. Lower-skilled jobs represent a major part of the employment which will be created in the next decade, just as they were over the last decade. Many of these jobs are necessary both for the individual workers, for their livelihoods, and for the economic and social success of the country. However, it will not be enough simply to deregulate employment in the hope that more low-wage employment can be created, because much of the lower-skill employment and self-employment being created is inadequate on a number of counts. In many cases, it is inadequately remunerated for the employees who take the work to generate independent life chances for themselves. The negative results of this are twofold, first many potential workers are discouraged from taking up employment, because they cannot survive on it. This implies the need to think again about the costs of working for low wages, and about the existing poverty traps. Second, rates of pay which are inadequate to establish an independent life can prevent young people from leaving home and carrying on a normal life pattern, with potentially serious economic consequences for parent, child and society in years to come.

Lower-skill work is often also inadequate because it provides no skills upgrade path, thus work becomes dead-end and frustrating. The changing skill requirements towards the need for self-motivation, communication skills and so on are rarely in themselves recognised as skills. The lack of appropriate training in these dimensions is one aspect of the problem and possibly a greater realisation of the need for these skills and the potential to certificate them for all workers could increase their explicit value. However, it is likely to be the case that even where formal skills enhancement takes place, paper qualifications from established educational institutes are likely to be regarded by organisations as the only legitimate claim on a progressive career. Increasingly, it seems that access to the career ladder is via a bachelor's degree or more.

References

Appelbaum E and P Albin (1989) 'Computer rationalisation and the transformation of work: lessons from the insurance industry'. In *The Transformation of Work*, ed. S Wood. London: Unwin Hyman

Atkinson J, 'Literacy Difficulties and the Labour Market: Swimming Against the Tide,' paper given at Employment Service Research Conference, Sheffield, March 1992, cited in Meager and Williams op.cit.

Beynon H and T Nichols (1977) *Living with Capitalism*. London: Routledge and Kegan Paul

Corocan T, G Hughes and J Sexton (1993) *Occupational Employment Forecasts 1996*. Dublin: FAS/ESRI

Ducatel K and I Miles (1995) 'The End of the Cinderella Syndrome? Service Innovation in the information Economy'. In *Technology Management*, ed. L Lefebvre. London: Paul Chapman Publishing

ECSC-EEC-EAEC (1993) *Growth, Competitiveness, Employment. The Challenges and Ways Forward into the 21st Century*. White Paper, Bulletin of the European Communities 6/93. Brussels

Freeman C and L Soete (1994) *Work for All or Mass Unemployment? Computerised Technical Change into the 21st Century*. London: Pinter

Holmes B (March 1989) 'Literacy and Numeracy: What Cause for Concern?' *Employment Gazette*, pp.133-139

Meager N (1994) 'Does Unemployment Lead to Self-Employment?', *Small Business Economics*, vol.4, pp.87-103

Meager N, G Court and J Moralee (1994) *Self Employment and the Distribution of Income*. IMS Report No. 270, Brighton: Institute for Manpower Studies

Meager N and M Williams (1994) *The case for national equality in employment targets*. Brighton: Institute for Manpower Studies

MHA (1994a) *Unemployment in Croydon*. Croydon: Mark Hepworth and Associates and Croydon Council

MHA (1994b) *Small Firms in Croydon*. Croydon: Mark Hepworth and Associates and Croydon Council

Mingione E (1991) *Fragmented Societies*. Oxford: Basil Blackwell

Nelson K (1986) 'Labour demand, labour supply and the surburbanisation of low-wage office work'. In *Production, Work and Territory*, ed. A Scott and M Dear, pp.149-168. Hemel Hempstead: Allen and Unwin

Pahl R (1988) *The Division of Labour.* Oxford: Basil Blackwell

Prais S and K Wagner (1988) 'Productivity and Management: the Training of Foremen in Britain and Germany', *National Institute Economic Review,* 123:34-47

Rapp N (June 1991) 'Basic Skills at Work', *Employment Gazette,* pp.347-350

Rees T (1994) 'Information technology Skills and Access to Training Opportunities: Germany and the UK'. In *Employment and Technical Change in Europe,* ed. K Ducatel, pp.113-135. Aldershot: Edward Elgar

Richardson R (March 1994) 'Teleservice Cities? "Second Wave" Back Offices and Employment in European Cities'. Paper delivered at conference on 'Cities, Enterprises and Society on the Eve of the XXIst Century', Lille, France

Rubery J and C Fagan (1994) 'Women's Occupational Employment in the EU', *Bulletin on Women and Employment in the EU,* no.4, April 1994. Brussels, p.1

6 Can our education and training system deliver? Britain's comparative performance

Peter Robinson

There is a consensus across the political spectrum in Britain that the failings of the education and training system are a major contributor to Britain's economic problems. This view is based on a perception that the skills base of the British population is inferior when compared with that of other advanced industrial countries, and that this skills deficiency causes a low rate of economic growth and contributes to unemployment.

This chapter looks at comparable data on Britain and other advanced industrial countries. It concludes that, on the most comprehensive measures of skills attainment, Britain's skills base does not seem to be out of line with countries which have a similar standard of living, though there is a lag compared with countries which are significantly more affluent. This conclusion is contrasted with more pessimistic analyses, and reasons for these differing conclusions are discussed.

The chapter looks in turn at Britain's comparative performance in compulsory schooling, further education, and training for the employed labour force. (For a discussion on higher education, see Chapter 3.) The chapter points out that young people in Britain have been voting with their feet to stay on in full-time education post-16. Britain has evolved towards an 'American' model of college-based general education rather than a 'Germanic' model of employer-based vocational education.

To make confident statements about comparative performance relies on having comprehensive, comparable data. Typically, cross-country comparisons tend to involve only a handful of countries at a time, because most researchers lack the resources to access data for a wider range of comparisons. Data available from the OECD do not suffer from this problem but do need to be viewed with some caution, due to definitional differences. A key argument which underlies this chapter is that assessments of the relative performance of Britain's education and training system need to be based on systematic quantitative evidence for as wide a range of countries as possible.

Performance in compulsory schooling

The basic indicator of the performance of compulsory schools in England is the trend in O level/CSE or GCSE results. The replacement of O levels and CSEs by GCSEs renders longitudinal comparisons problematic.[1] In the summer of 1987 just over 26 per cent of 16 year olds achieved five or more higher-grade passes under the old style examinations. The introduction of GCSE saw a sharp increase to over one third by 1989. Since then there has been a steady rise in the proportion of 16 year olds obtaining five or more higher grades to over 43 per cent by the summer of 1994.

Comparison of performance with other countries is rendered difficult due to the absence of data on more than a few countries. The National Commission on Education presented data which showed 16 year olds in England performed poorly compared with those in Germany, France and Japan (Table 6.1) (National Commission, 1993). However, these data may not be strictly comparable.[2] Perhaps a better comparison for England might involve taking the NVQ level 2 benchmark (that is the equivalent of five GCSEs at grade C

Table 6.1
Proportion of 16 year olds achieving a broadly comparable qualification in 1990-91

percentages

Germany	62
France	66
Japan	(50)
England (GCSE A-C English, maths & science)	27

Note	Germany – proportion passing the *Realschulabschluss* or proceeding to the *Abitur;* France – proportion passing the *Brevet*.
Source:	Green and Steedman, 1993, Table 1

or above), achieved by 42 per cent of 16 year olds or, alternatively, the figures for passes in English and mathematics, achieved by 50 per cent and 37 per cent respectively (Department for Education data). On these measures the achievement of English 16 year olds still lags behind, but to a lesser degree, that of those in France and Germany.

An alternate basis for comparison are internationally administered tests in mathematics and science. These were most recently administered to samples of young people in a wide range of countries in 1991. Table 6.2 shows the average scores in the mathematics component for ten countries. A critical point stressed by the OECD is the need to recognise that many of the differences between countries are not statistically significant – they could have arisen randomly. The results for England are especially problematic because the sample from that country was the smallest. This is why the table shows that the average mathematics score for 13 year olds in England was not significantly different from any other country, with the exceptions of Switzerland, where scores were significantly higher, and Portugal, where scores were significantly lower. In Scotland 13 year olds also performed significantly less well than Swiss students, but better than 13 year olds in the US, Spain and Portugal. As can be seen the mean score for Scottish students was exactly equal to the mean score for English students. The only reason we can say that Scottish students did significantly better than those in the US and Spain, and English students did not, is because the sample of Scottish students was over twice as large and therefore comparisons can be made with more confidence. The 1991 test showed that the range of attainment in mathematics for English students was broadly similar to the average spread of scores for the better and poorer performing students in the other countries (Table R2(B), OECD 1993).

Table 6.3 reports the results of the science component of the test administered at the same time as the mathematics component in 1991. This shows 13 year olds in England and Scotland scoring significantly less well than students in Switzerland, and significantly better than students in Ireland and Portugal, with the differences compared with all the other countries not statistically significant.

These results then do not show that 13 year olds in England and Scotland in 1991 were greatly out of line in terms of their attainment

Future skill demand and supply

Table 6.2 Overall student proficiency in mathematics at age 13 in 1991

Sample	Sample size	Mean score	Switzer-land	France	Italy	Canada	Scot-land	Eng-land	Ireland	Spain	US	Portugal
Switzerland	2738	70.8		+	+	+	+	+	+	+	+	+
France	1760	64.2	−		=	=	=	=	=	+	+	+
Italy	1478	64.0	−	=		=	=	=	=	+	+	+
Canada	2590	62.0	−	=	=		=	=	=	+	+	+
Scotland	1547	60.6	−	=	=	=		=	=	+	+	+
England	704	60.6	−	=	=	=	=		=	+	=	+
Ireland	1638	60.5	−	=	=	=	=	=		+	=	+
Spain	1487	55.4	−	−	−	−	−	−	−		=	+
US	1329	55.3	−	−	−	−	−	=	=	=		+
Portugal	1502	48.3	−	−	−	−	−	−	−	−	−	

Notes: Reading across for each country, a + sign indicates that the mean score for that country was significantly higher than in the comparison country; a − sign indicates that the mean score was significantly lower; an = sign indicates that the mean scores in the two countries were not significantly different from one another.
Only 15 cantons were sampled in Switzerland. The sample for Italy came from Emilia-Romagna. The sample for Spain excludes Catalonia.

Source: Table R2 (A), OECD, 1993

Can our education and training system deliver?

Table 6.3 Overall student proficiency in science at age 13 in 1991

Sample	Sample size	Mean score	Switzer-land	Italy	Canada	Eng-land	France	Scot-land	Spain	US	Ireland	Portugal
Switzerland	2738	73.7		+	+	+	+	+	+	+	+	+
Italy	1478	69.9	–		+	+	=	=	=	=	+	+
Canada	2590	68.8	–	–		=	=	=	=	=	+	+
England	704	68.7	–	–	=		=	=	=	=	+	+
France	1760	68.6	–	=	=	=		=	=	=	+	+
Scotland	1547	67.9	–	=	=	=	=		=	=	+	+
Spain	1487	67.6	–	=	=	=	=	=		=	+	+
US	1329	67.0	–	=	=	=	=	=	=		=	=
Ireland	1638	63.3	–	–	–	–	–	–	–	=		=
Portugal	1502	62.6	–	–	–	–	–	–	–	=	=	

Notes: See notes to Table 6.2.

Source: Table R3 (A), OECD, 1993

in mathematics and science when compared with most of the other countries which participated in the study.[3] Only Swiss students did consistently and significantly better.

In conclusion, the most comprehensive data on the level of attainment in basic subjects towards the end of compulsory schooling, does not put British students significantly behind those in most other countries.

Participation and performance in further education
Traditionally the single most important emphasis in the debate on the relative performance of the British education system has been on the failure of that system to offer either universal full-time education, or vocational education and training by firms, to the majority of young people as they reach the end of compulsory schooling.

In the late 1980s Britain was almost unique among advanced industrial countries in not having the bulk of its 16 and 17 year olds in full-time education or training. At the time, it was predicted that without major efforts at reform, this situation would persist. Ironically, at the very time this was being argued the situation was being transformed.

Since 1986-87 staying on in full-time education in England post-16 has increased sharply (Figures 6.1 and 6.2). By 1993-94 72 per cent of 16 year olds were still in full-time education in the January following their exit from compulsory schooling, compared with 45 per cent in 1986-87 (Figure 6.1). Some three-fifths of 17 year olds in 1993-94 were still in full-time education 18 months after leaving compulsory schooling, compared with 35 per cent in 1986-87 (Figure 6.2). It is not a gross exaggeration to describe these trends as a transformation, although by 1994-95 this increase had come to a halt.

In 1993-94 about one quarter of all 16 and 17 year olds were enrolled in full-time education, while simultaneously holding a part-time job. Only an estimated 6-7 per cent of 16 year olds and 17-18 per cent of 17 year olds were in regular full-time jobs. Around 13-14 per cent of both age groups were reported to be in Youth Training (YT). A worrying residual were unemployed or inactive – some 6-7 per cent of 16 year olds and around 10 per cent of 17 year olds.

The Youth Cohort Studies (YCS) suggest that around half of those 16 year olds in full-time jobs in 1991-92 were receiving off-

Can our education and training system deliver?

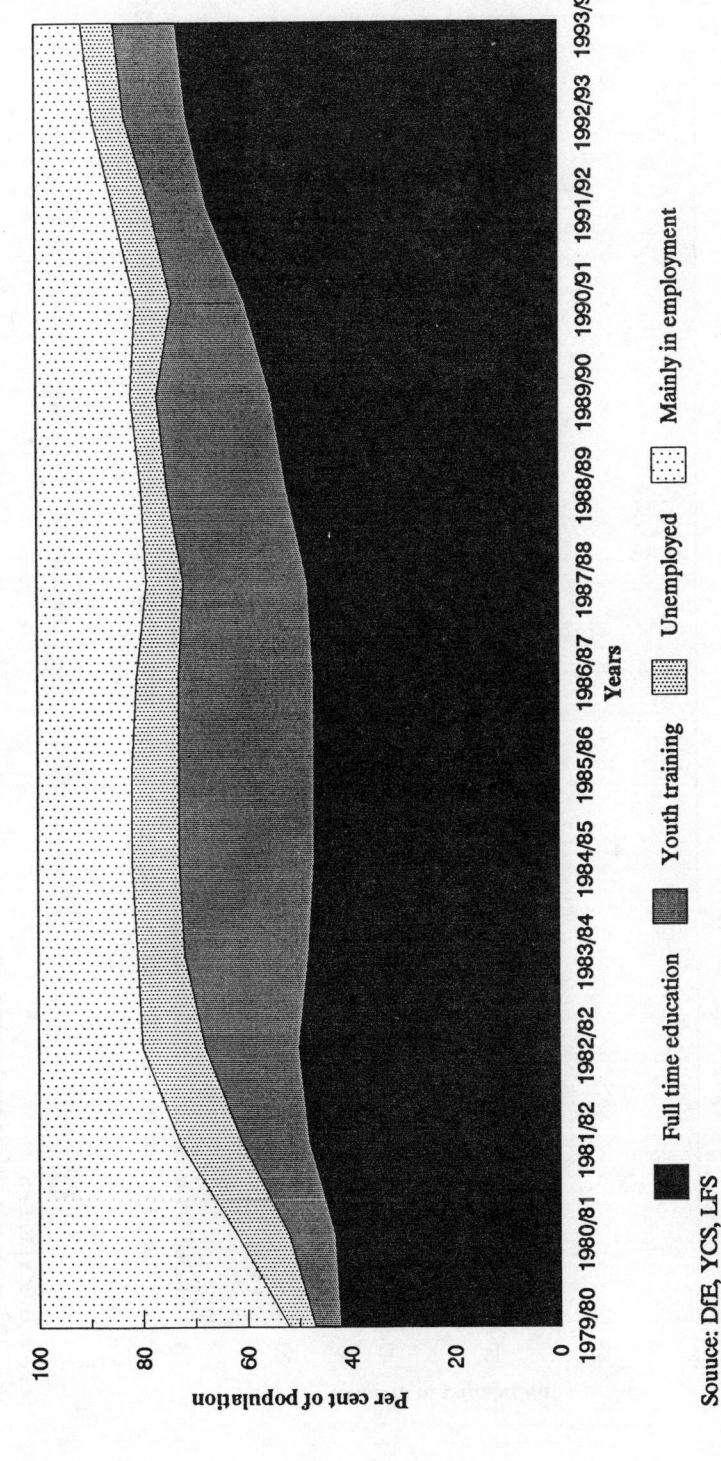

Figure 6.1 Educational and economic activity of 16 year olds in England, 1979/80 to 1993/94

Source: DfE, YCS, LFS
Note: The category 'mainly in employment' is a residual and includes a small number inactive

Figure 6.2 Educational and economic activity of 17 year olds in England, 1979/80 to 1993/94

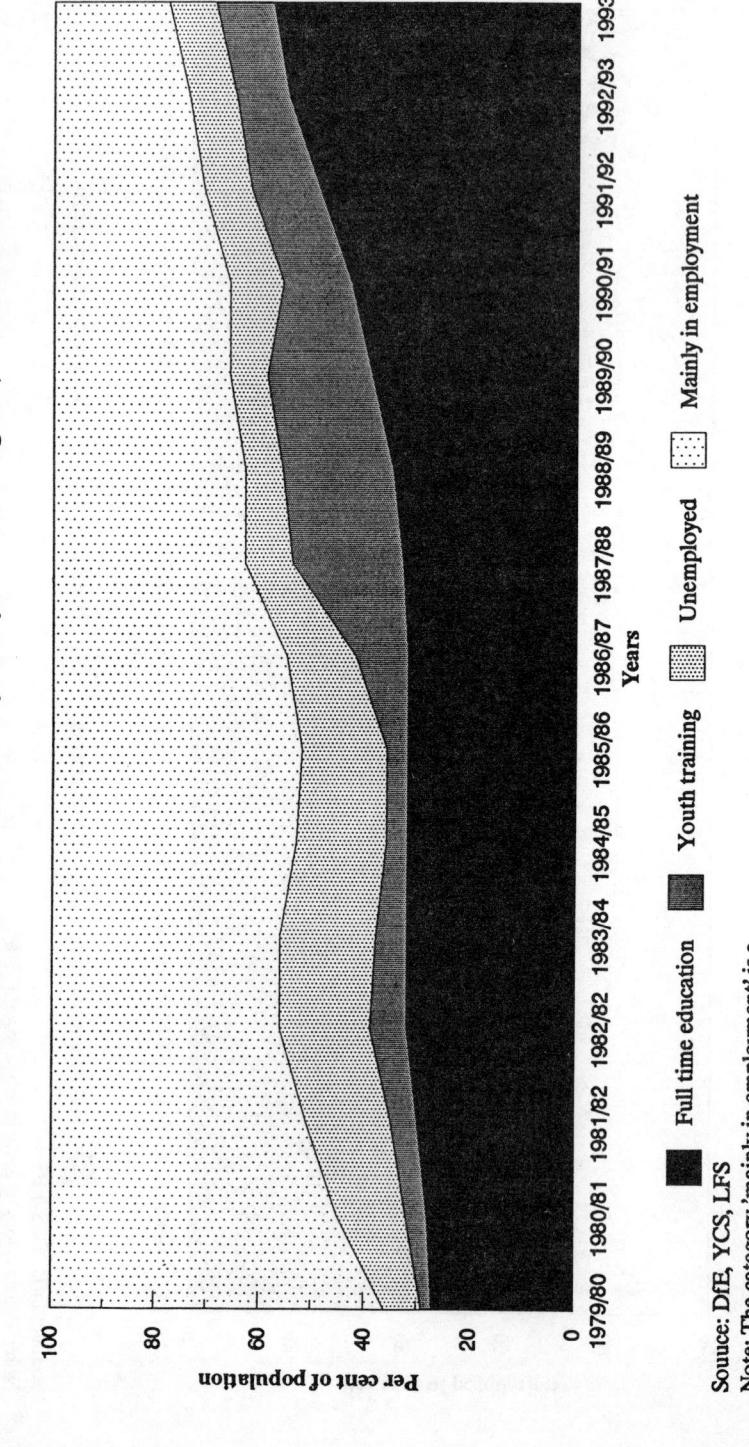

Source: DfE, YCS, LFS
Note: The category 'mainly in employment' is a residual and includes a small number inactive

the-job training, as were nearly three-fifths of 17 year olds in full-time jobs. These figures represented significant improvements in the incidence of off-the-job training when compared with previous years, though matched curiously by a fall in those reporting on-the-job training (*Employment Gazette,* May 1993).

It still needs to be emphasised that around half of those 16-17 year olds in full-time work, at least half of those on YT, as well as the worrying residual who were unemployed or inactive in 1993-94, were still receiving little or no further education and training of a recognised standard. These groups probably summed up to around 15-20 per cent of 16/17 year olds and one quarter of 17/18 year olds in 1993-94.

Figure 6.3 summarises data on the participation of 16 and 17 year olds in full-time education and training in the OECD in 1991. Most countries have been increasing enrolment and in 1991 an average of around 90 per cent of 16 year olds and 80 per cent of 17 year olds were enroled in either full-time general or vocational education or in apprenticeship-based schemes in the OECD countries. England, with four-fifths of 16 year olds and two-thirds of 17 year olds enrolled in similar provision in 1993, continued to trail, but the extent of convergence since 1988 is significant.

The increased staying on rate in England has not led to a greater proportion of students enrolling on less advanced courses, in fact quite the opposite, as a higher proportion of 16 year olds who stayed on in the early 1990s enrolled straight onto A level or advanced vocational courses. In autumn 1993 45 per cent of all 16 year olds enrolled onto these advanced courses compared with just 25 per cent in 1986. In the summer of 1993 just over 24 per cent of 18/19 year olds had achieved two or more A level passes compared with 14 per cent in 1987. When those achieving equivalent vocational qualifications are added, then in 1993 37 per cent of those aged 21-23 in Britain had achieved NVQ level 3 qualifications, that is two A level passes or their equivalent (NACETT, 1994). Between 1988 and 1993 the proportion of young people enrolling in higher education doubled from 15.1 per cent to 30.9 per cent. This expansion in higher education enrolment at age 18/19 closely correlates, with a lag of two years, with the increase in the staying on rate at age 16.

For 1991, Figure 6.4 shows the proportion of young adults aged 20-24 in each country which had not completed 'upper secondary'

Future skill demand and supply

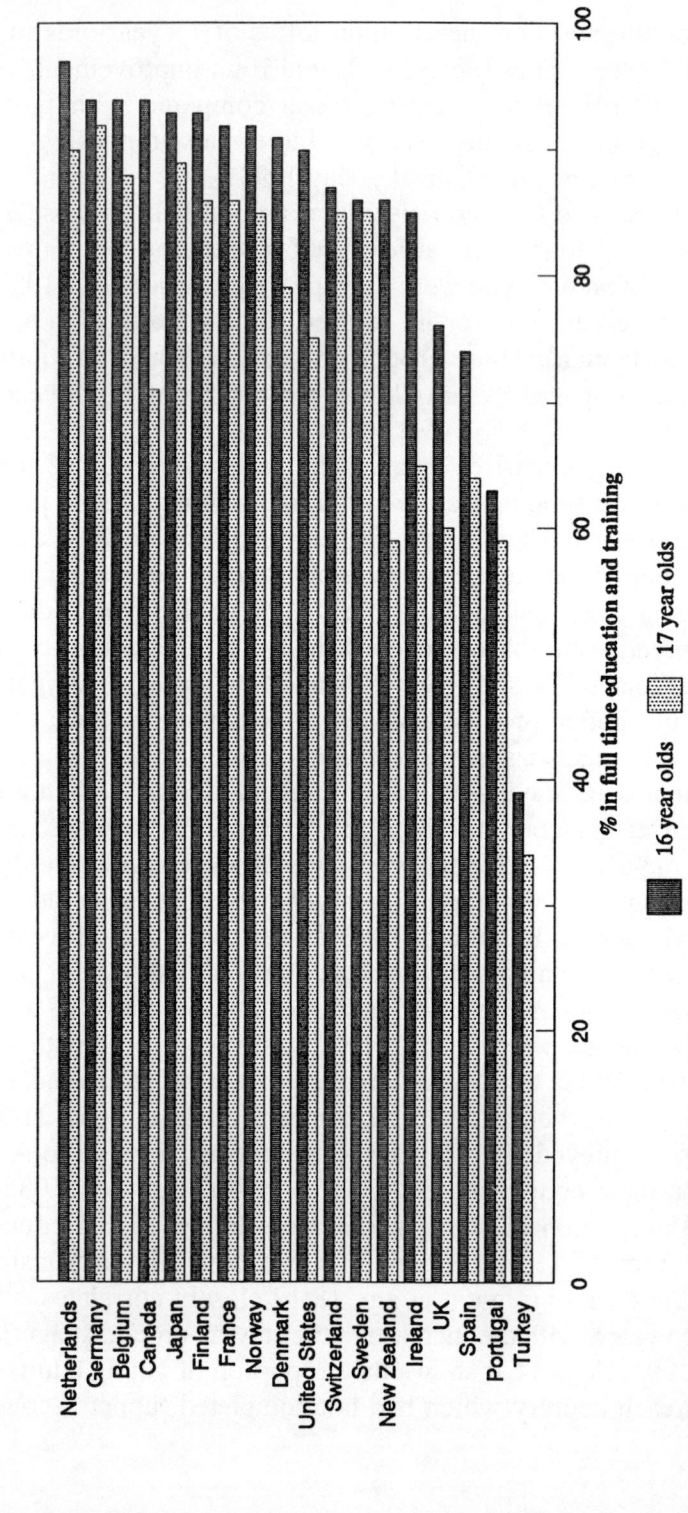

Figure 6.3 Participation in full-time education and training, 1991

Source: Table P13(A), OECD 1993 and DfE 10/94.
Notes: Full time equivalents enrolled in general and vocational education and apprenticeships.

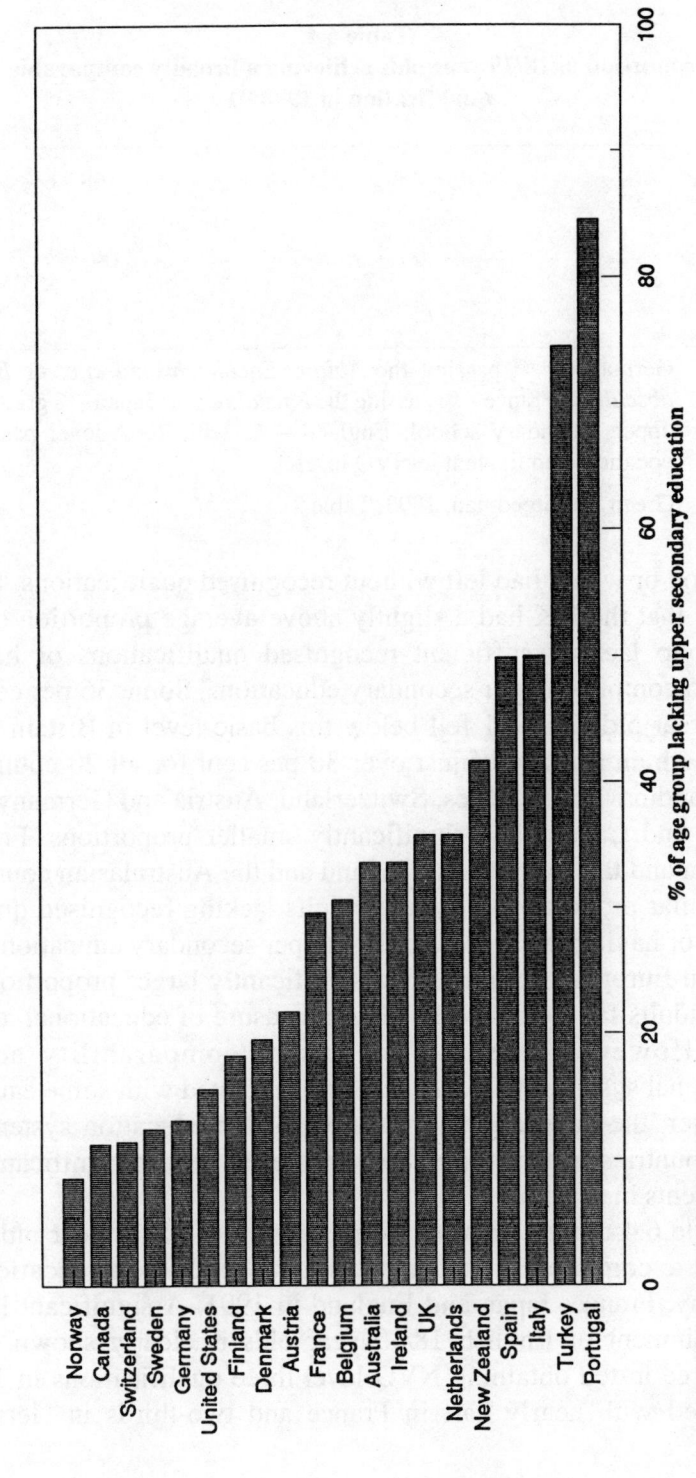

Figure 6.4 Basic educational attainment of the population aged 20-24 in 1991

Source: Table 1.C.1, OECD 1994
Note: Proportion below ISCED level 3: refer to text for discussion of what this measure means.

Table 6.4
Proportion of 18/19 year olds achieving a broadly comparable qualification in 1990/91

percentages

Germany	68
France	48
Japan	(80)
England	30

Note   Germany – % passing the *Abitur, Fachhochschulreife*, or *Berufsabschluss;* France – % passing the *Baccalaureat;* Japan - % graduating upper secondary school; England – % with 2+ A-level passes or vocational equivalent ie NVQ level 3.

Source: Green and Steedman, 1993, Table 2

education or which had left without recognised qualifications. It can be seen that the UK had a slightly above average proportion of the age group lacking sufficient recognised qualifications or having failed to complete upper secondary education.[4] Some 36 per cent of 20-24 year olds in 1991 fell below this basic level in Britain compared with an average of just over 30 per cent for all 20 countries. The Scandinavian countries, Switzerland, Austria and Germany, and the US and Canada had significantly smaller proportions. France, Belgium and the Netherlands, Ireland and the Australasian countries had similar proportions of young adults lacking recognised qualifications or having failed to complete upper secondary education. The southern European countries had significantly larger proportions of young adults falling below this basic measure of educational attainment. However, due to problems of comparability across educational systems, this data needs to be treated with some caution. Moreover, the data reflects the output of the education systems in these countries in the mid-1980s, before the recent significant improvements in Britain.

Table 6.4 reports data on the proportion of 18/19 year olds obtaining a comparable upper secondary school qualification in Germany, France, Japan and England in 1991. A significant lag in the attainment of English 18/19 year olds is clearly shown, with only three in ten obtaining NVQ level three qualifications in 1991, compared with nearly half in France and two-thirds in Germany achieving a broadly comparable level. The figure for Germany is made up of 32 per cent obtaining the *Abitur* or a vocational qualification in full-time education, and 36 per cent obtaining an apprenticeship by this age.

These results are broadly consistent with the OECD data based on the proportions of young people falling below the International Standard Classification of Education (ISCED) level 3 (Figure 6.4). Young people in Germany, for example, were clearly significantly better qualified on average than young people in Britain in the early 1990s, regardless of the measure used. A broadly similar proportion in both countries obtained the equivalent of 2 A level passes or a pass in a full-time vocational education course, but in Germany this was matched by as big a proportion again obtaining an apprenticeship. It is thus the output of the German apprenticeship system which counts in making up the difference between the attainment of young adults in Britain and Germany.

A further common criticism of the advanced qualifications aimed at by 18/19 year olds in England is their narrow focus. Students usually study only three A levels. In all other countries students follow a much broader course of study, including ongoing formal tuition in mathematics and the home language. Any comparison involving any number of countries would call into question this narrow focus of the A level examinations system. There are also legitimate concerns about the quality of some of the intermediate and advanced vocational qualifications on offer in Britain.

To conclude, the most comprehensive measures of the proportion of the population obtaining some kind of school leaving qualification in 1991 did suggest that Britain had some catching up to do. A somewhat higher proportion of young people in Britain in 1991 lacked sufficient recognised qualifications when compared with the average for other countries, and the quality and breadth of some of those qualifications could be questioned. However, as a result of sharply increased staying on rates since 1988, Britain is probably closing the gap.

Training for the employed
It is frequently asserted that British firms carry out less training than firms in other advanced industrial countries. In fact the high quality

Future skill demand and supply

Figure 6.5 Proportion of employees receiving job-related training in last four weeks before the survey, 1984-93

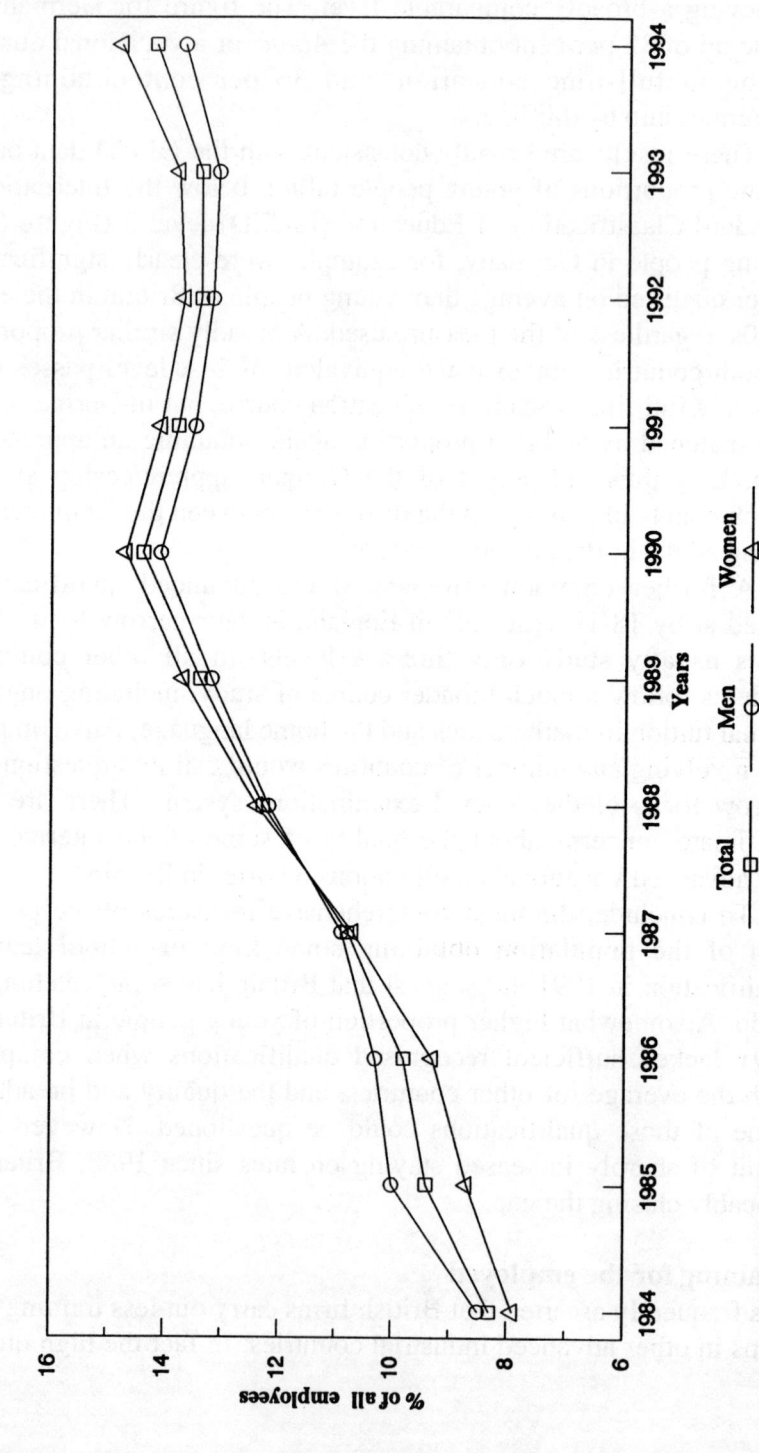

Source: Labour Force Survey, Spring

Table 6.5
Incidence of training among employees as measured by labour force type surveys

	Date of survey	Reference period for training	Proportion of employees reporting any training
Britain	1989	Last four weeks	14.4
Germany	1989	Last four weeks	12.7
Ireland	1989	Last four weeks	7.8
Spain	1990	Last four weeks	2.4
Sweden	1987	Last five months	25.4
France	1989	At the time of the survey	4.6
Australia	1989	Last 12 months	79.0
Finland	1987	Last 12 months	34.4
US	1989	Since the job was obtained	35.8

	Proportion of employees reporting training by age					
	15/16-19	20-24	25-34	35-49	50+	All
Britain	23.0	19.4	16.0	13.3	7.2	14.4
Germany	75.9	19.8	8.0	3.5	..	12.7
Ireland	28.0	13.6	6.2	3.5	1.7	7.8
Spain	5.8	5.4	3.3	1.0	0	2.4

Source: OECD, 1991, Table 5.1a

data needed to support or refute such an assertion is simply not available.

Figure 6.5 shows the results from the British Labour Force Survey (LFS) which measure the proportion of employees who reported receiving job-related training in the four weeks leading up to the survey. This proportion grew steadily over the period 1984-90 and then slipped slightly during the recession, before recovering again. The data represents a modest indication of an improvement in the incidence of training available to British employees. However, the figures give no indication of the quality or effectiveness of that training, or whether it involves work towards any recognised qualifications. It is a very basic indicator of the incidence of training.

Table 6.5 shows data on the incidence of training reported by employees in other countries measured in a similar way to those presented for Britain in Figure 6.5.[5] The lower part of Table 6.5 focuses on the four countries with the same reference period for the surveys, that is those employees who reported receiving training in the four weeks prior to the survey. What is striking is that a slightly higher proportion of employees reported receiving training in Britain than in Germany, and significantly more in Britain than in Ireland or Spain. The age breakdown shows the high reported incidence of training for teenagers in Germany due to the apprenticeship system. Young adults aged 20-24 in Britain and Germany were equally likely to report receiving training. Adults aged between 25-49 in Britain were over twice as likely to report having received training in the previous four weeks as their counterparts in Germany.

These results, of course, go against the grain of most assumptions about Britain's relative training performance. However, the limitations of the data must be emphasised. The OECD stressed strongly that the data for making adequate cross country comparisons in the area of the provision of training by firms was too weak to support anything other than 'conjecture' about the relative performance of different countries (Chapter 5, OECD 1991). The data may reflect different interpretations of what constitutes training. They reveal nothing about the duration or quality of the training or its effectiveness. They are only very crude indicators of the incidence of training. Therefore, at most, it can be concluded that the information relating to Britain's relative performance is contradictory and that it cannot be assumed that Britain definitely lags.

The overall stock of skills in the population

It should be clear on the basis of the data presented that assertions that the British education and training system is inferior in all respects cannot be supported by a detailed analysis of the available information. An overview of the outputs of the system as a whole in terms of the overall stock of skills in the British adult population also would not support such an assessment.

Figures 6.6 and 6.7 present data on the overall stock of skills in the adult populations of the OECD nations. Figure 6.6 measures the proportion which did not complete upper secondary schooling or left

Can our education and training system deliver?

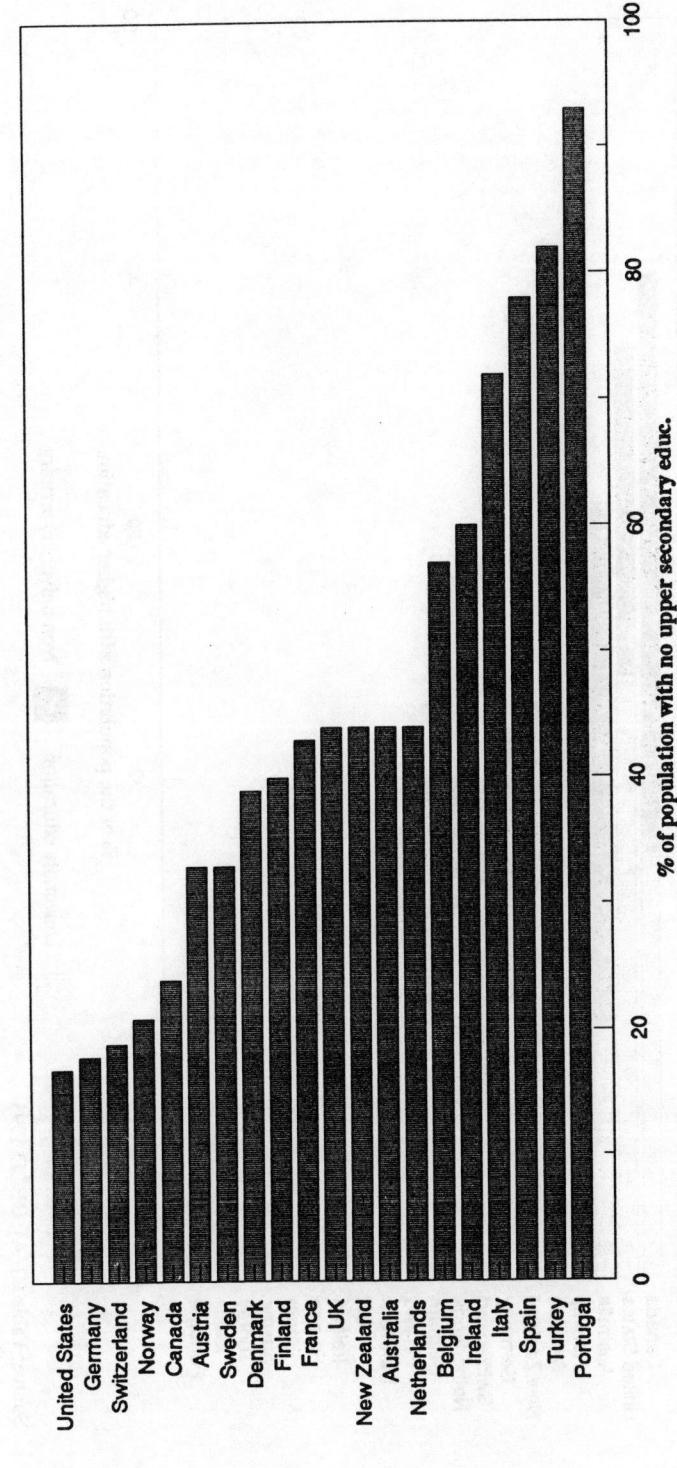

Figure 6.6 Basic educational attainment of the population aged 25-64 in 1991

Source: Table C1(A), OECD, 1993
Note: % below ISCED level 3: refer to the text for discussion of what this measure means.

Future skill demand and supply

Figure 6.7 Higher educational attainment of the population aged 25-64 in 1991

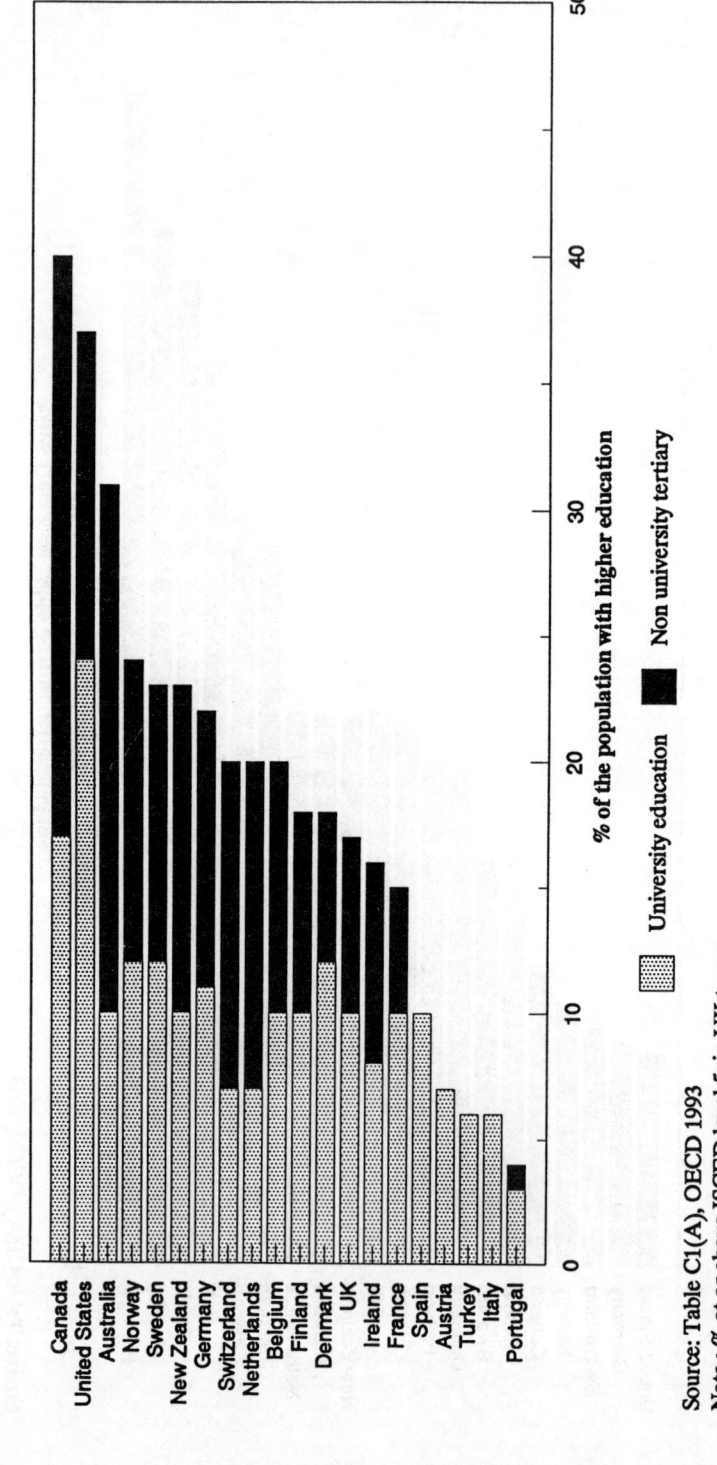

Source: Table C1(A), OECD 1993
Note: % at or above ISCED level 5: in UK terms all those with post A level qualifications

Can our education and training system deliver?

with no recognised qualifications.[6] Figure 6.7 shows the proportion of the population with all higher education qualifications acquired at university or in non-university higher education. In the countries with the highest per capita GDP (the USA, Canada, Germany and Switzerland), the vast majority of the population have recognised qualifications, acquired through compulsory education, and post-compulsory schooling (the USA and Canada) or apprenticeship training (the Germanic countries) (Figure 6.6). The USA and Canada also have a large proportion of the population with higher education qualifications (Figure 6.7). This is not true for the Germanic countries, but the quality of the technical skills acquired through the apprenticeship systems in those countries means that the average skills attainment of the population is still very high.

What should be clear about Figures 6.6 and 6.7 is Britain's position in the middle ranking of countries. In 1991 Britain had an average proportion of the population lacking sufficient recognised basic qualifications, an estimated 44 per cent as against an average for all countries of 45 per cent. Britain had a slightly below average proportion of the population with all forms of higher education in 1991, 16 per cent as against an average of 19 per cent in the OECD. However, if non-university higher education is excluded (the darkly shaded parts of the bars in Figure 6.7) then the proportion of the British population with university higher education (10 per cent) was at the OECD average. Overall then, on these measures, Britain was generally not out of line with other countries which have similar standards of living in terms of the stock of skills in the population.

Figure 6.8 shows that there is an especially good correlation between the level of basic skills in the adult population and the level of per capita GDP. The most successful industrial countries have only small proportions of the population lacking basic skills. Relatively poorer economies such as those in southern Europe have a much larger proportion lacking basic skills. The UK is firmly planted in the middle ranking of countries. Italy is the real outlier with a large proportion of the population lacking basic skills as in other southern European countries, but with a level of per capita GDP in line with other middle ranking states.

Figure 6.9 shows a poorer correlation between the attainment of higher educational qualifications and economic performance.[7] Countries such as Canada and the USA have high levels of higher

Future skill demand and supply

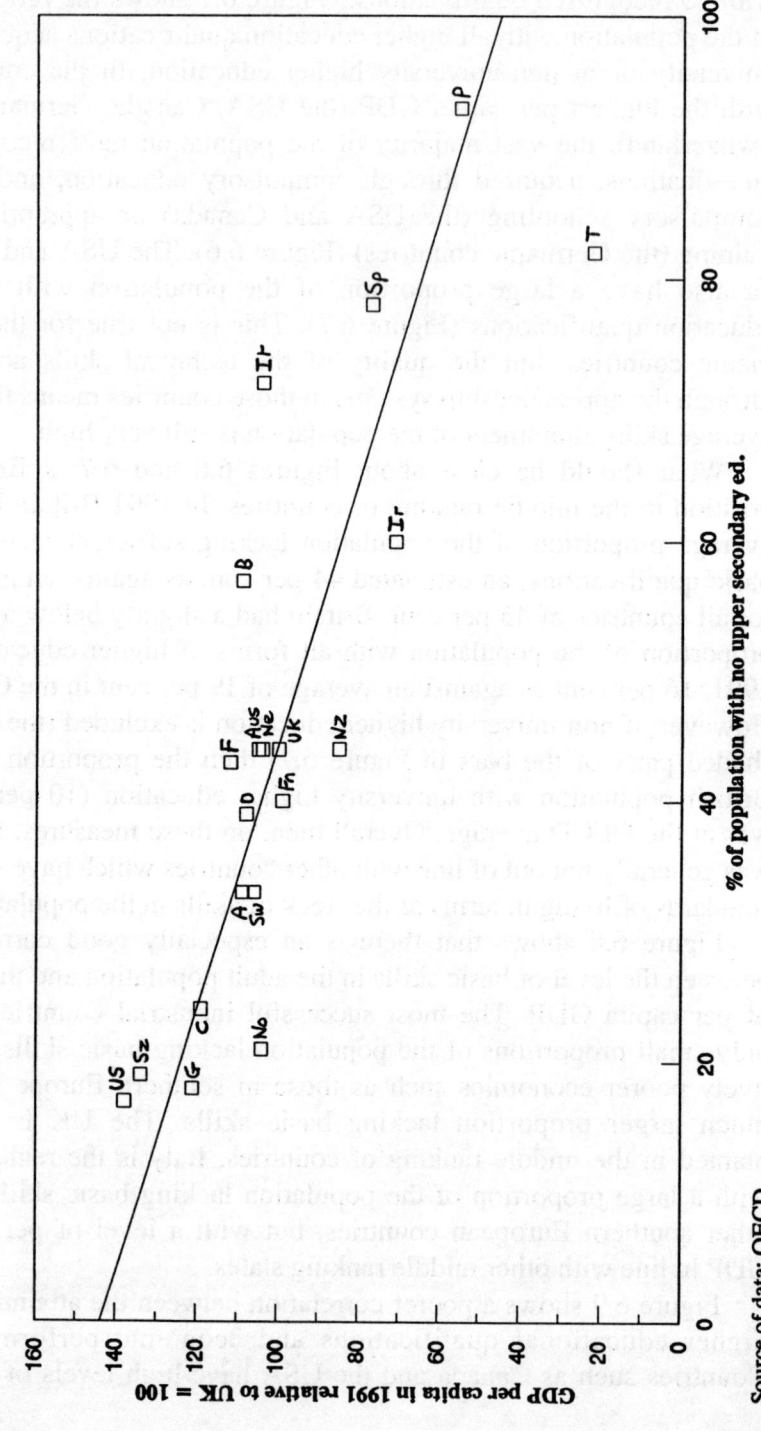

Figure 6.8 Living standards and basic educational attainment in 1991

Can our education and training system deliver?

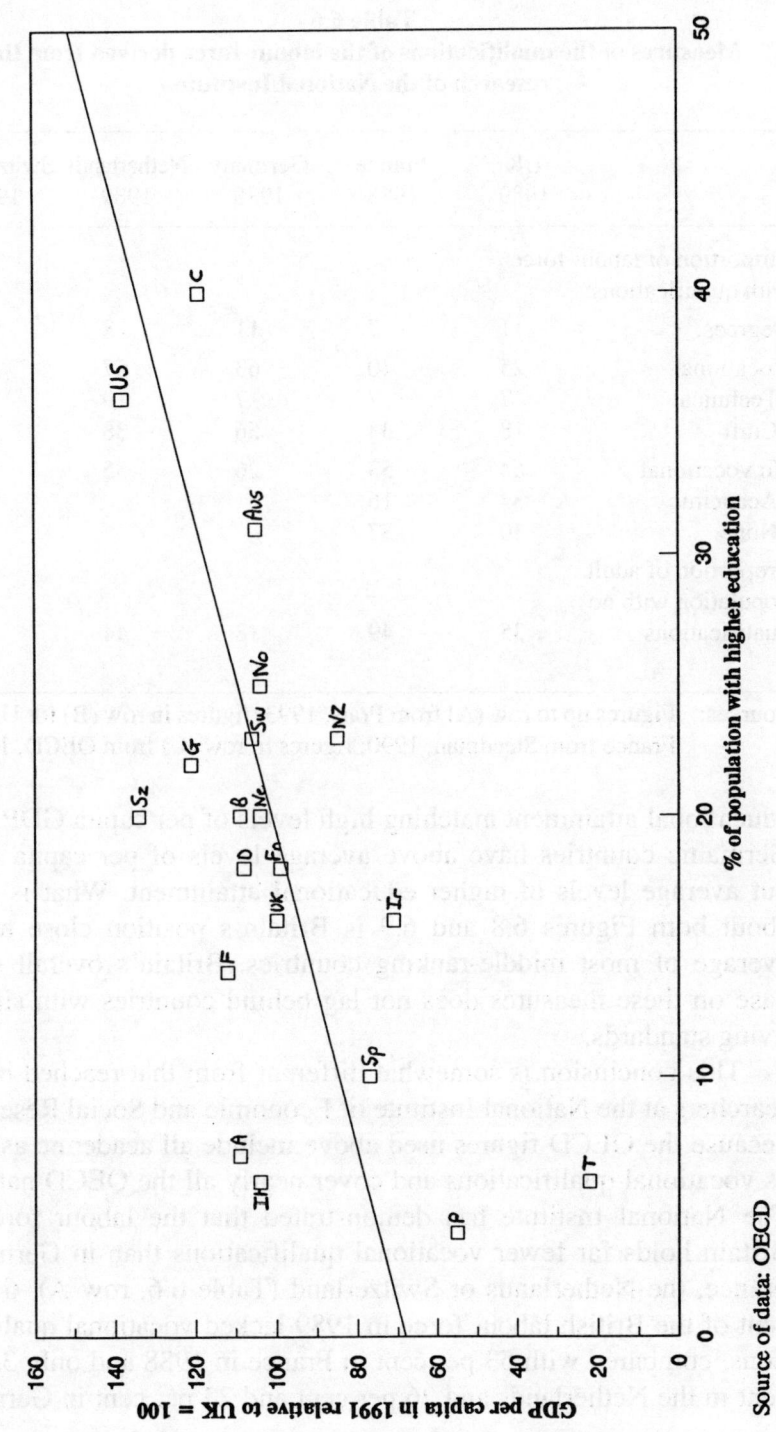

Figure 6.9 Living standards and higher educational attainment in 1991

Source of data: OECD

Future skill demand and supply

Table 6.6
Measures of the qualifications of the labour force derived from the research of the National Institute

	UK 1989	France 1988	Germany 1988	Netherlands 1989	Switzerland 1991
Proportion of labour force with qualifications:					
Degrees	11	7	11	8	11
Vocational	25	40	63	57	66
- Technical	7	7	7	19	9
- Craft	18	33	56	38	57
No vocational	64	53	26	35	23(A)
- Academic	34	16			
- None	30	37			(B)
Proportion of adult population with no qualifications	35	49	18	44	19(C)

Sources: Figures up to row (A) from Prais, 1993; figures in row (B) for UK and France from Steedman, 1990; figures in row (C) from OECD, 1993

educational attainment matching high levels of per capita GDP. The Germanic countries have above average levels of per capita GDP but average levels of higher educational attainment. What is clear about both Figures 6.8 and 6.9 is Britain's position close to the average of most middle-ranking countries. Britain's overall skills base on these measures does not lag behind countries with similar living standards.

This conclusion is somewhat different from that reached by researchers at the National Institute of Economic and Social Research, because the OECD figures used above include all academic as well as vocational qualifications and cover nearly all the OECD nations. The National Institute has demonstrated that the labour force in Britain holds far fewer vocational qualifications than in Germany, France, the Netherlands or Switzerland (Table 6.6, row A). 64 per cent of the British labour force in 1989 lacked vocational qualifications, compared with 53 per cent in France in 1988 and only 35 per cent in the Netherlands and 26 per cent and 23 per cent in Germany and Switzerland respectively, at similar points in time. However, if all academic qualifications are counted then according to the National Institute the relative positions of Britain and France would be reversed, with 37 per cent of the French labour force lacking any qualifications as against 30 per cent of the British labour force. This would be consistent with the rankings produced by the OECD data. Consideration of all academic qualifications would also probably equalise the ranking of Britain and the Netherlands in Table 6.6, though Germany and Switzerland would continue to register a significantly smaller proportion of the workforce lacking any qualifications. If countries such as the USA and Canada were included in Table 6.6 then the proportion of their labour forces lacking vocational qualifications would probably approach 50 per cent, as the majority of those without higher education in these two countries hold high school graduation certificates, essentially an 'academic' qualification. If Italy were included the proportion of the labour force lacking vocational qualifications would probably be around 75-80 per cent.

Conclusions
A significantly smaller proportion of the British labour force holds vocational qualifications when compared with four other western European nations. When compared with 19 other OECD countries, and counting all qualifications, the proportion of the British population lacking any qualifications in 1991 was at about the average for these countries. The proportion of the British population holding higher education qualifications was slightly below the average if all higher qualifications are included and at the average if only university higher education is included. Using the most comprehensive measures of skills attainment across a wide range of nations, the overall stock of skills in the British population does not seem to be out of line with countries which have a similar standard of living, though there is a lag compared with countries which are significantly richer in terms of per capita GDP.

The debate on education and training in Britain needs to reflect the fact that a great deal has changed since the late 1980s. Young people have voted with their feet to enter further and higher education in significantly greater numbers. This means that Britain has evolved towards the 'North American' model with high levels of full-time participation in post compulsory education, rather than a 'German' style employer-based route for teenagers. Nearly three-quarters of 16 year olds stayed on in full-time education in 1993/94 and a quarter of 16-17 year olds in 1993/94 were in full-time education while holding a part-time job – very much the American model of combining education with some work experience and income from the regular labour market.

The kind of 'skills revolution' which many observers were arguing for in the late 1980s has to a certain extent occurred. The national targets which were originally set in the early 1990s for increasing the proportion of the age group achieving advanced qualifications and enrolling in higher education have either been met (the higher education target) or look like being met by the end of the decade. A range of issues relating to the quality and breadth of British qualifications remains to be addressed, but there should be more than a begrudging admission of the progress which has been made. Given this, and given the uncertain nature of the evidence purporting to show a *causal* link between educational attainment and economic performance, the continued heavy focus on education and training as the number one priority for public policy in Britain looks more like a desire to avoid having to give full weight to other issues of importance to our economic performance, which may be more pressing, but which are also more complex and more controversial.

References

Department for Education (1994) 'Participation in Education by 16-18 year olds in England: 1983/84 to 1993/94', *Statistical Bulletin,* 10/94, July

Employment Gazette, 'What happens to young people after 16: new results from the Youth Cohort Study', vol.101, no.5, May 1993

Green A and H Steedman (1993) *Educational Provision, Educational Attainment and the Needs of Industry: a review of research for Germany, France, Japan, the USA and Britain,* Report Series No.5. London: National Institute of Economic and Social Research

National Advisory Council for Education and Training Targets (NACETT) (1994) *Report on Progress.* London

National Commission on Education (1993) *Learning to Succeed.* London: Heinemann

OECD (1991) *Employment Outlook.* London: HMSO

OECD (1992) *Education at a Glance: OECD Indicators.* London: HMSO

OECD (1993) *Education at a Glance: OECD Indicators.* London: HMSO

OECD (1994) *Employment Outlook.* London: HMSO

Prais S (1993) *Economic Performance and Education: The Nature of Britain's Deficiencies.* Dicussion Paper No.52, London: National Institute of Economic and Social Research

Steedman H (1990) 'Improvements in Workforce Qualifications: Britain and France 1979-88', *National Institute Economic Review,* August

Notes

1. The first full cohort of examinees sat GCSEs in 1988.
2. The figures for both Germany and France are based on post-16 qualifications which require written examinations in mathematics and the home language, but not in science, so that the level of science attainment is unclear. The comparability of the Japanese and English data is also unclear, as the derivation of the Japanese data is not given and the authors emphasise that Japan has no national school leaving examinations.
3. This casts further doubt on the comparability of the data in Table 6.1, as it seems unlikely that the deterioration in comparative performance over three years could be so great.
4. The published OECD figures for Britain seem too generous, including as they do individuals with just one or two O levels. The data used in this chapter attempt to adjust for this probable over-estimation of the British skills base. The data for Britain in Figure 6.4 correspond approximately to the proportion of young adults who had failed to attain qualifications at around NVQ level 2 in 1991.
5. The information is drawn from labour force-type surveys and measures the proportion of employees who reported receiving training during some specified time period before the survey was conducted. As these reference periods vary from survey to survey Table 6.5 needs to be read with considerable caution.
6. The data for Britain have been adjusted to include those with only one or two O levels.
7. An important qualification to Figures 6.8 and 6.9 is that they do not prove that higher skills attainment *causes* a country to have a higher per capita GDP. The correlations reported might simply imply that more affluent countries can afford to give their populations greater access to education.

7 Training policy for competitiveness: time for a new perspective?

Ewart Keep and *Ken Mayhew*

During the last decade there has apparently emerged in British policy-making circles what might be dubbed a post-Reichian consensus about the key role that skill enhancement plays in international competition. Reich's thesis (1983) that the skills of the workforce, whether at company or nation state level, will be the chief determinant of international competitive advantage has been accepted by the National Commission on Education, the Commission on Social Justice, the Confederation of British Industry, the Trades Union Congress, the Institute of Directors, the government, and by Labour and the Liberal Democrats. Allied to this is a general belief that Britain has a problem with the current skill levels of its workforce, and with the provision of vocational education and training (VET) – a view reinforced by comparative research (O'Mahoney, 1992; Prais, 1990; Worswick, 1985). These concerns, it should be noted, are simply the latest manifestation of worries about the unsatisfactory state of skills in Britain – the perception of which has waxed and waned over the last century and a half (Perry, 1976; Reeder, 1981).

It is apparent that, with the exception of a few dissenting academic voices (Cutler, 1992; Pratten, 1990; Shackleton, 1992), there is broad agreement that we have a problem. There is even a consensus about the answer – measures to boost the supply of education and training, with the belief that more and better education and training will produce positive economic and social results for individuals, employers and the economy as a whole. As a result, policy has, and appears likely in the future, to concentrate on initiatives aimed at improving the supply of skills, such as youth training

(YTS/YT), modern apprenticeships, youth credits, Investors in People (IIP), the creation of a 'training market', the National Education and Training Targets (NETTs) and so on. The vision that underpins these policies, particularly the NETTs, is one that sees the adoption of competitive strategies based around higher skill levels and high quality goods and services as inevitable across the whole economy and labour market.

However, supposing we have misdefined the nature of the problem, or at least looked at only one part of the problem's causation? If we have, there is a strong likelihood that the policy that has been prescribed to tackle it will not produce optimal results. More and better VET is not an end in itself. It will only produce a worthwhile payback if the skills that are created are needed and can be utilised. Put simply, our argument is that as well as possible problems with skill supply, Britain has traditionally experienced a simultaneous problem of weak demand for skill. This weak demand has, at least in part, been the cause of many of the difficulties with skill supply. Furthermore, the high skills vision may only apply to some sectors of the economy and some parts of the labour market. In others, at least in the short to medium term, different routes to competitive advantage are being and will be pursued.

This chapter seeks to explore this proposition. We look first at the evidence that demand for skills is limited within the British economy. The reasons for weak demand are outlined, and there then follows an exploration of some of the avenues available to policy-makers in seeking to tackle this complex and deep-seated structural problem.

Some evidence for limited demand for skills
Glynn and Gospel (1993) point to historical evidence that weak demand for skills from employers has been a recurrent element in the structural configuration of the British labour market since the late nineteenth century. There are indications that the problem is still with us.

Reactions to the NETTs
To begin with, the reaction of many employers and some sectors of employment to the NETTs, particularly to the targets for lifelong learning, suggests that the vision of a skilled workforce that the

targets embody is at variance with the reality of future skill needs in some workplaces and sectors. Two sectors – hotels and catering, and construction – have decided that the current targets of half the workforce aiming towards NVQs by 1996, and half the workforce qualified to NVQ level 3 by the year 2000, are unrealistic, and have set themselves informal targets at half these levels. The printing industry, the seventh largest UK manufacturing industry, is aiming for 25 per cent of workforce qualified to NVQ level 3 by 1998. These sectors represent a substantial workforce (hotels and catering account for about one in ten of the employed population).

The payback to investment in training
A second cause for concern about demand is the limited payback to investment in skills by individuals, both in terms of financial reward, and the often weak influence of formal skills and qualifications on the recruitment and selection process. Bennett, Glennerster and Nevison suggest that the returns to post-compulsory education and training are at best mixed, and that the relatively low level of VET in Britain 'is not primarily the result of supply constraints, but is caused by a low level of demand' (1992, p.15). Differentials between skilled and unskilled workers are often weak (Steedman, Mason and Wagner, 1991), and the Challenge to Complacency study concluded that 'pay and status are rarely linked to the attainment of qualifications or attendance at training courses' (Coopers and Lybrand, 1985, p.13). Moreover, the importance afforded to the possession of formal skills and qualifications in the selection process, whether for initial employment or for promotion, is in some cases uncertain (see, for example, Employment Department, 1991; Collinson, 1988).

Skill demand in NVQs
Another indicator that demand for high levels of skill may not be universal among British employers comes from the new qualifications structure. When some employers have been given the opportunity, via NVQs, to help design qualifications that meet their skill requirements, the standards that have been set have often proved to be low, at least by contemporary European standards (Prais, 1989 and 1991; Smithers, 1993).

The fate of YTS/YT

The most significant item of evidence for limited demand for skills comes however, from the fate that has overtaken many recent attempts to boost the supply of VET. To take YTS/YT as an example, YTS was intended to 'become a permanent feature of vocational education and training provision in this country' (Employment Department, 1985, p.7), to revolutionise both the quality and quantity of initial vocational training for young people, and thereby create the foundations upon which a more highly qualified and adaptable workforce could be built. In the event, employer-provided training of uniformly high quality and status was not forthcoming, and YTS/YT has failed to gain permanence, or to change fundamentally the attitudes of many employers towards the provision of training for young people (see Keep, 1994, for details).

Thus, in 1990 only a third of YT trainees had employed status, and Labour Force Survey data for 1991/92 suggests that, of the 284,000 16 and 17 year olds in employment, no more than 100,000 were receiving training (including YT) (National Commission on Education, 1993, p.276). Moreover, despite having been in operation, in one form or another, for more than a decade, in 1993/94 only 42 per cent of YT trainees achieved an NVQ of any sort. Even this low pass rate is 28 per cent better than the figures for 1992/93 (*Times Higher*, 2 September 1994). This improvement has been brought about, not by increasing employer demand for better qualified young workers, but by the imposition by government of outcomes-related funding for YT. Payment-by-results has forced employers and other training providers to make greater efforts to gear training to qualifications.

Other parts of the training system have also encountered problems caused by limited employer demand. The collapse of the traditional apprenticeships, the failure of schemes aimed at introducing German 'meister'-style qualifications for British supervisors, the persistent inability of programmes aimed at re-skilling the adult unemployed (such as Employment Training (ET) and Training for Work (TfW)) to provide training that leads to a qualification, and the slow take-up of IIP and NVQs, all point to, at best, patchy demand for a skills revolution.

Skill shortages

A number of pieces of what might be regarded as countervailing evidence need to be addressed. First, there have been some suggestions that skill shortages are starting to re-emerge as the economy moves out of recession. We need to be clear that these skill shortages represent the difficulties which some employers face in recruiting pre-trained and qualified staff. These recruitment difficulties can stem from a number of factors, of which an inadequate supply of skills is but one (Green and Ashton, 1992; IFF, 1994; Lam and Marsden, 1992). Other causes include inadequate levels of pay and poor working conditions, a reluctance by employers to train their existing staff, and attempts by employers to shift the responsibility for and cost of skills acquisition back into the education system. At present, recruitment difficulties tend to be concentrated in sectors and occupations that have problems over relative levels of pay and working conditions, such as catering, textiles, health ancillaries, and nursing (IFF, 1994).

Qualification levels demanded of job applicants

Second, there is evidence (Employment Department, 1993 and 1994; Gallie and White, 1993) that the level of qualifications required by employers from job applicants is rising. This, it is suggested, is clear proof of a general rise in demand for skills. However, changing entry requirements, do not, of themselves, necessarily mean that the skill level needed to undertake the job has changed. Employers may simply be using higher qualification levels as a screening device to limit the number of job applications, or reacting to rising levels of participation in post-compulsory education. For example, with the massive increase in higher education, graduates are now entering jobs in retail and banking that a decade ago would have been occupied by A level school leavers. The skill demands of the job may not have risen, but employers have traded up their entry requirements, partly because of the prestige that attaches to employing graduates, but also because the A level leavers they formerly employed are no longer there – they are staying on into higher education.

Demand for skills across the economy – a complex picture

Finally, we would emphasise that we are not suggesting that demand from employers for skills and qualifications is uniformly low across the entire economy, or that overall skill requirements within the labour market may not be rising. What we do argue is that there are a significant number of sectors of the economy, a substantial group of employers, and a variety of occupations, where skill demands are and will remain low. In these parts of the British economy skills supply is currently broadly in line with skills demand, and consistent with the competitive strategies being pursued by employers in those firms and sectors. This situation serves to depress aggregate demand for skills and qualifications, and weakens the effective operation of the training market.

One factor that helps obscure this problem deserves to be highlighted. The use of the phrase 'demand for skills' and/or qualifications often conflates demand from individuals to acquire skills and/or qualifications, and demand from employers for those possessing them. Thus, the Confederation of British Industry (1994a) in calling for a further expansion of higher education, suggests that this be 'demand led'. In this case, the demand being referred to was that from individual prospective students for places in HE, rather than, and independent of, any clearly identified requirement from employers for more graduates. At present, and for the foreseeable future, the supply of graduates exceeds demand from employers for those with such qualifications (Court, Connor and Jagger, 1994).

There is undoubtedly strong evidence that, particularly among young people, there is a strong demand for qualifications. This demand is reflected in the very rapid take-up of GNVQs, and by the large scale expansion of participation in higher education. Whether the perceptions of the future of the labour market that is fuelling this demand by individuals actually accords with the likely pattern of skills and qualifications required by employers, remains to be seen. At some levels it may do so. Enhanced qualifications may not produce increased pay or career prospects for young people, but, as suggested above, may be a prerequisite for access to scarce employment opportunities. Whether, in cases where employers are bidding up entry requirements, but not upgrading significantly the nature of the jobs, the skills of the individual will be put to productive use remains questionable. It is difficult to see how sectors such as hotels and catering, whose current demands for skills appears low (Price, 1994), and whose job structure provides little opportunity for progression and careers (Metcalf, 1988; Price, 1994), will be able to absorb profitably many of the 30,000 or so students currently studying for GNVQs in 'leisure and tourism'.

The factors that underlie weak demand for skills

The chief factors that underlie weak demand for skills fall into two groups. The first relates to the operation of the labour market and the management of the employment relationship. The second, to wider aspects of the economic structure in Britain, and the competitive strategies adopted by employers. In the space available, the analysis of these factors is necessarily brief. For a fuller treatment, see Keep and Mayhew (forthcoming a).

The British labour market and personnel management

Shifts in employment structure

Turning first to the nature of the British labour market and personnel management practices, it is apparent that current shifts in sectoral and occupational structures do not aid moves towards a uniformly highly-skilled workforce. A process of bifurcation appears to be under way. While professional/managerial employment is forecast to rise, so too is part-time work in low-skill areas such as personal and protective services (Employment Department, 1993; Rajan, 1993). The middle way of skilled manual occupations appears set to continue in relative decline (Employment Department, 1993). At the same time, areas of employment where training (and in some cases skill needs) have normally been lower than average – such as small firms, self-employment, and part-time employment – have been growing. This trend looks likely to persist. The Employment Department has commented that

> if there is an increase in part-time working, self-employment, employment in small firms and/or sectors with a traditionally low level of training activity, a concerted effort will be required to encourage an expansion in training activity. [Employment Department, 1993, p.60]

Training policy for competitiveness

The impact of a growing peripheral workforce
Allied to the above, the use of the core/periphery vocabulary, if not of the concept in any genuinely strategic sense (Hakim, 1990) has meant that many employers have shifted an increasing proportion of those they employ into what they perceive as the periphery (part-time work, fixed-term contracts, etc). This trend appears likely to continue. A recent Institute of Management survey of long-term employment strategies suggested that nearly 70 per cent of respondents expected the use of temporary workers to increase over the next four years, and 60 per cent expected that a quarter of their employees would be complementary to the core workforce within four years (Institute of Management, 1994).

The implications for skills and training are worrying. Part-time work is heavily concentrated in lower-skill, lower-status occupations (Dex, 1988). Part-timers are less likely to be trained than full-time workers (*Labour Market Quarterly Report,* February 1993, p.6), and only 47 per cent of employers recruiting temporary and casual workers provided them with training, as compared to 71 per cent for all recruits (IFF, 1994). The CBI has acknowledged these concerns, admitting that 'employers report they are less prepared to train their part-time, and, in particular, temporary staff than they are to train their full-time and permanent employees ... where training does take place for flexible workers this is, in many companies, restricted to a minimum' (CBI, 1994b, p.7); and has concluded that, 'there are ... indications of actual or potential market failure in the training provision required for flexible workers' (CBI, 1994b, p.33).

Thus, changes in the labour market are busy reducing the proportion of the workforce in the type of jobs (full-time, permanent) for which investment in training is most easily supported by employers. An increasing percentage of the workforce are now employed on terms and conditions that implicitly reflect a reduction in their employers' commitment to offer them training and development.

The weak take-up of 'soft' human resource management (HRM)
The increasing use of casualisation, usually driven by a desire to reduce short-term employment costs, in part reflects the difficulties experienced by many British employers in actually putting into practice the rhetoric of developmental styles of human resource management. Evidence from large-scale surveys and case studies

(Whipp, 1992; Millward et al, 1992; Millward, 1994; Edwards et al, 1992; Sisson, 1994; Marginson et al, 1993), suggests that a widespread adoption of the sophisticated HRM model has not taken place in this country. Many companies have dabbled with isolated elements of HRM, but a coherent and sustained approach has been lacking (Edwards et al, 1992).

Furthermore, in sectors where traditional collective bargaining has declined, it has not been replaced by well-thought out strategies for employee involvement, but by greater informality in the management of the employment relationship (Millward et al, 1992). In many firms, workers, far from being treated as a resource, are regarded simply as a commodity or 'factor of production'. (Millward, 1994), and Sisson (1994, p.41) concludes that 'the likelihood is that, for the average UK employee, the experience of personnel management in Britain in the mid-1990s is less like the "HRM organisation" than it was a decade ago'. Yet, without personnel management systems capable of capturing the motivational benefits of training, or of creating forms of job design and work organisation that can provide opportunities for greater worker autonomy and the utilisation of higher levels of skill, demand for increased skills will be limited, and the deployment of existing skills to maximum effect will be harmed. As a study commissioned by the Information Technology Association of Canada (Verma and Irvine, 1992) underlines, the linkages between HRM, work organisation, social partnership and employee involvement, and high levels of skill are clear. Creating, sustaining, and productively deploying a highly-qualified workforce is problematic except in the supportive context of a high-quality system of personnel management.

Perhaps most worryingly of all, there is some evidence that even when delivering a relatively high specification service, like personal banking, British employers seek to do so using more Tayloristic forms of job design and work organisation than some of their European counterparts, with the result that skill levels in the British banks are lower (O'Reilly, 1992; Anderson, 1994). There have also been instances where despite all the good intentions of the HRM model of personnel management being present, companies have in reality reduced employee discretion over the work process and allowed low-trust employee relations practices to thrive (Sewell and Wilkinson, 1992; Delbridge and Turnbull, 1992).

Economic structure and its effects upon competitive strategy

The second set of factors that appear to limit the demand for skills are bound up with structural developments in the British economy, and their effects upon choice of competitive and product market strategy.

Dwindling commitment to the domestic economy

The commitment towards and investment in the British economy by many large 'British' firms is dwindling. Of the *Times* Top 100 companies for the year 1989/90, at least 17 employed the majority of their workforce abroad, and many others were moving in this direction as investment overseas has increased. For example, in 1987, UK companies spent $31.7 billion in the USA alone (Rogers and Tran, 1988). In the manufacturing sector, this has meant investment in the creation of skilled jobs abroad, rather than within the domestic economy. Although inward investment, for example from Japan, has helped balance this outflow of capital (and associated jobs), during the 1980s as a whole outward investment exceeded inward investment by a ratio of slightly more than two to one. These developments mean that some major British firms now have domestic operations that are a shrinking and increasingly marginal proportion of the whole. As a result, investment in these parts of the business, and in their workforces, may cease to be a priority. Also, insofar as an employer-led training system has meant one led by large companies, who have traditionally provided the bulk of formalised training (Finegold, 1992), a weakening commitment to the UK economy on their part must raise doubts about the viability of this strategy.

Short-termism

Argument still abounds as to the degree to which the failure of British companies to adopt a strategic approach to personnel management, and to invest in R&D and training is a consequence of short-term pressures generated by the structure of finance capital, and by the City's concern for short-term profit maximisation (Walker, 1985; Cosh et al, 1990; RSA, 1994; Marsh, 1990; CBI, 1987; Hutton, 1995). Contrasts have recently been drawn (RSA, 1994) between the Anglo-Saxon model of short-term capitalism, in which the interests of the shareholder are the sole and over-riding concern, and 'stakeholder' capitalism (such as is found in Japan, Scandinavia and Germany), where a longer-term perspective and a wider range of interests (such as those of employees) inform the corporate decision-making process.

Whatever the strength of the case for a problem with short-termism engendered by the City, and the balance of the argument does appear to have swung in favour of this proposition, there is very strong evidence that in many companies the mechanisms of managerial control 'peer at the business through numbers' (Goold and Campbell, 1986) and encourage a short-term perspective on internal investment decisions (Marsh, 1990). The effects on personnel management have been to hinder the adoption of a strategic approach (Purcell, 1989), and often to encourage a concentration on labour cost containment at the expense of investment in improving the 'performance capacity of labour' (Hyman, 1992 p.17).

The structure of domestic demand
Another constraint on overall skill needs is the structure of the domestic economy in the UK economy. This limits the market for high quality goods and services that require a high-skill input. The UK contains one in five of the EU's poor (Commission on Social Justice, 1993, p.22), and 10 of the UK's 11 regions have a gross domestic product per head of population lower than the EU average. The number of people living on less than half average income in the UK has risen from three million in 1977 to 12 million in 1988/89 (Goodman and Webb, 1994). There are an estimated 12.5 million adults and children (20 per cent of the population) living on weekly incomes below income support levels or less than £10 above it (*The Guardian,* 17 April 1993). Within such an economy, competition based on the price, rather than the quality of goods and services, will remain an important consideration.

Product market strategies
In the light of the above factors, which weaken the ability of many British employers to make major upward adjustments to their skill requirements, much of the British economy may be trapped in a 'low skills equilibrium' (Finegold and Soskice, 1988). There is evidence that at least some sectors are concentrating on low-specification, low-cost, standardised goods and services that create a

weak demand for additional skills (Prais, 1990; New and Myers, 1986, Reich, 1983). In terms of the changing balance between imports and exports, British manufacturing appears to be doing better in low-tech areas, such as slaughtering and meat processing, and parts of the food industry; and less well in high-tech, high-skills production in engineering and electronics (Temple, 1994; Oulton, 1993; Katrak, 1982). Buxton, Mayers and Murfin (1994, p.147) suggest that Britain has, in relative terms, been moving towards 'a less skilled, less technically intensive product mix'.

These product market strategies feed back into work organisation and job design, and from thence into the poor take-up of the soft or developmental version of HRM. As Lloyd and Rawlinson (1992) suggest, sophisticated HRM techniques may be applicable only in circumstances where the product market strategy requires 'workers who have jobs that are or could be redesigned to engender commitment and individual initiative' (1992, p.189). In sectors such as the clothing industry, product market strategies based on low-cost mass production, de-skilling, and Tayloristic methods of job design and work organisation, mean that these conditions rarely exist (Lloyd and Rawlinson, 1992; Harijan, 1991).

Factors curtailing demand – some general comments
Besides the fact that many of the issues outlined above fall outside the terms within which the British training debate has traditionally been framed, there are two general points which need to be made. First, that a voluntaristic, employer-led training system faces severe problems when employers, through resort to a crude core/periphery model, are actively minimising their commitment to an increasing proportion of the workforce. Both the CBI and the TUC have recently acknowledged the importance of this issue (Industrial Relations Research Unit, 1994; CBI, 1994b).

Second, that the broad context within which these factors have been operating is one where the government has been attempting the simultaneous pursuit of two competing visions of the labour market and of competitive advantage. Government has promulgated measures to create a de-regulated labour market, and accepted the argument that low wage costs and a highly de-regulated labour market can provide a major source of competitive advantage (Employment Department, 1988; DTI, 1991). According to the

OECD, Britain, along with the USA, now possesses the most deregulated labour market in the developed world (OECD, 1994) The government appears to have found it hard to appreciate the effects that such a labour market would have on skill utilisation, and ultimately, upon the success of measures to boost skill supply

By contrast, when it has come to pondering the Reichian vision of competitive advantage, policy-makers have given every appearance of accepting the requirement for more and higher levels of skill and for their application in pursuit of higher-spec, higher-value added competitive strategies, but tended to underestimate the barriers that moves towards the creation of a casualised, de-regulated labour market might put in the way of realising this goal. The implicit assumption has been that demand for more and better skills would arise automatically in response to inexorable competitive pressures, and could be left to take care of itself.

This belief has in many cases proved to be false. In particular, the attractiveness to many British employers of the potential alternative competitive strategy offered by the exploitation of a traditional route of increased labour intensification, reduced wage costs, and casualisation of employment, has been underestimated. Confronted by the two inherently competing visions of the future being offered by official policy, a considerable number of employers have opted for the one with which they are most familiar. Rather than proceed along the route leading to a high-spec, high-value added, high-skills product market strategy, supported by a strategic, 'soft' HRM approach to employee commitment, motivation and reward, many employers, have preferred to stick with what they know best, and to concentrate on work intensification, headcount reductions, new forms of Taylorism, and crude 'hire and fire' employment practices (Millward et al, 1992; Sisson, 1994).

Enhancing demand for skills – a different vision of policy
Faced with this analysis of the nature of the training problem, four reactions are possible. One is simply to reject the analysis, and to argue that problems with demand for skills are a relatively minor factor within Britain's training problem.

A second response is to accept that problems may exist on the demand side, but argue that the pursuit of competitive strategies based on factors other than skills are rational in both the short and long terms, and that the decisions of individuals and companies, operating within labour and training markets, must, because of the intrinsic nature of the market mechanism, produce optimal economic results. Intervention to tackle limited demand is therefore unnecessary, and indeed would prove counterproductive, as it would impede the free operation of the market. From this perspective, it can be argued that current training policies are proving successful. If the aim of policy is to produce amounts of skill that will meet present and likely future demand, based upon current competitive strategies and the continuation of established labour market developments, it would seem that policy has achieved its goal. Any problems at the margin with unsustainable competitive strategies and a failure to deploy skills to maximum productive effect, will be dealt with by competitive pressures, which will force companies to change.

A third reaction is to acknowledge difficulties with weak demand, but to try to tackle them through the supply side of the equation. Boosting the supply of skill, particularly through the education system, it is argued (Soskice, 1993), can over time alter the ways in which employers design jobs and utilise the capacities of their workers, influence competitive strategies, and thereby increase the productive use of skills and boost demand for VET.

The final reaction, which is the one which we seek to explore below, argues that none of the above responses is satisfactory, and that direct interventions to boost demand for skills are a necessary precondition for securing a widespread and lasting solution to the training problem. Before examining this approach to policy, the potential weaknesses of the other responses needs to be outlined. First, the evidence for problems with skills demand, particularly in some parts of the labour market, is compelling and should not simply be ignored.

In relation to the market-based approach, we would argue that, given the scale, persistence, and mutual reinforcement of the deep-seated structural factors impeding moves towards a high-skill, high-productivity, high-wage economy, there must be doubts that market forces alone will prove sufficient to move significant parts of the economy in this direction. For example, Price (1994) demonstrates the difficulties that confront the hotel and catering sector in seeking to improve personnel practices without the aid of external pressure and intervention. Furthermore, markets are prone to failure, and when faced by some of the intractable structural constraints discussed above, the chances of such failure increase. The CBI recognises this difficulty in relation to 'flexible' workers (CBI, 1994b). Thus structural developments in the labour market and the economy produce powerful forces that may shape, rather than be shaped by, decisions about VET. Moreover, as evidenced above, the danger of relying solely on the current battery of labour market and training policies, is that the mixed messages they send may be encouraging some employers to run ever-faster down the cul-de-sac of a competitive strategy based on low labour costs.

Finally, what of arguments that the best way of attempting to boost demand for skills lies in increasing their supply? As mentioned above, recent years have witnessed a significant rise in staying-on rates at school, and in participation in higher education. This has led some authors (for example, Soskice, 1993) to suggest abandoning the employer-based route for initial VET and rely more upon the full-time education route to deliver a high-skills, high-quality economy.

Crudely put, the argument is that the choice of product and production strategy is a cost benefit analysis. The provision of more highly educated raw material significantly alters this calculus. Whether or not it alters it sufficiently for the purpose is a matter for conjecture. At best the case is unproven. We have the historical experience of the output of our education system improving more rapidly in quality than has the availability of jobs requiring higher level qualifications. The consequence of this, as has been outlined above, has been an occupational filtering down of graduates and others. Put differently, graduates today are doing jobs which graduates a generation ago would not have contemplated. What is lacking is firm evidence that their employers are offering them the scope to perform more effectively in such jobs than did their non-graduate predecessors. While such an approach might work in some sectors and with some employers, the barriers to progress outlined above suggest that in many instances it will fail, with the consequence that low-skill job design and work organisation will persist in many workplaces, and negative messages about the payback to investment in VET will filter back from the labour market to the education system.

Our response to the evidence that demand for enhanced skills is often lacking, is to contemplate policy interventions that would aim explicitly to increase demand for VET. Creating institutional mechanisms and relationships that can produce a greater supply of skills, knowledge, and the ability to apply them, is plainly a vital component of any successful training strategy. Nevertheless, it represents only one side of the equation. As has been outlined above, factors such as labour market structures and regulation, reward systems, work organisation regimes, job design, and the motivation and commitment of employees, will all affect the degree to which skills can be effectively allocated to and utilised within the productive process. These factors will also, over time, feed back into the training system, for example via the signals that reward structures send regarding the value placed on skill in a particular labour market, and therefore will have very significant effects upon the operation of the institutional mechanisms of skill supply. Hence these factors form a legitimate concern for training policy-makers, and it is our contention that a training strategy that fails to take these matters into account and to integrate them into the overall policy plan, runs the risk of encountering significant barriers to success. As Neale (1992, p.283) suggests:

> improved training may be a necessary condition of the sort of quality-led competitive strategies pursued by many German firms ... but there is little evidence that it is sufficient. Better training, by itself, does not transform industrial organisation.

If our diagnosis is correct – that structural factors impede moves towards a higher demand for skills in the British economy, and that the above responses to this situation are inadequate – what, if anything, can be done to change the situation, or at least ameliorate its worst effects? Diagnosis influences prescription. We have suggested that, rather than confronting the relatively simple difficulty of inadequate mechanisms of skill supply, the real problem may centre on the interaction between the institutional configuration of the labour market, the structure of economic activity, and weaknesses in individual companies, particularly with regard to job design and work organisation – an interaction that results in limited demand for skills, and consequently an often unsatisfactory payback to those who invest in skill acquisition. Such a diagnosis contains elements of systems failure.

This has important implications, both for the types of policy that might be adopted to tackle the problem, and for the processes by which such policies might be devised. If the basic problem is systemic, and extends well beyond inadequacies in skill supply, then the scope of policy analysis broadens, and with it the series of topics that policy must address. Furthermore, there will be a need to investigate and unpick the often complex linkages between the various casual factors.

Before examining what avenues are available for progress, we would wish to underline our belief that no easy or swift solutions are immediately obvious. The nature of deep-seated systems failures is that no single policy is likely on its own to be sufficient to have anything other than marginal impact. Equally some possible policy responses would involve a degree of intervention that contemporary political ideology would probably find unacceptable. Besides the underlying complexity of the problem, many developments that took place during the 1980s have created an environment hostile to a skills-rich competitive strategy for the whole British economy.

Some elements of this environment can be altered. Others are less tractable, for example, the problems of short-termism, and of the net outflow of capital from Britain. This development reflects a number of forces that are acting upon companies, such as the need to get closer to the market, particularly the fastest growing markets (which are outside the UK); and also the need to spread risk in the face of the continuing volatility of the domestic economy. Short of re-imposing exchange control regulations (which is rendered problematic by the provisions of the Single European Market), it is hard to see how this development can be slowed, let alone halted. Attracting more inward investment may help, but the problem of a net outflow of capital and of the increasing marginalisation of UK-based manufacturing operations in many large British-owned companies is likely to persist.

These difficulties accepted, where might a different approach to policy take us? Outlined below are some basic avenues for creating policies aimed at stimulating demand for skills.

A common vision of society

A prerequisite for progress is a broader view of the nature and causes of our training problem, and a willingness to contemplate a step change in policy rather than further incremental change. Our starting point is the need to develop a clear vision of how we wish our society to develop, and of the nature of relations which we wish to exist between those responsible for economic development.

The reinvention of a common view of society is important, simply because the outright denial by government of society's existence as a useful concept during much of the 1980s, has tended to encourage behaviour on the part of some actors which while logical from their individual perspectives, produces sub-optimal results for society as a whole. The growth of a casualised, peripheral workforce, at least partially excluded by their employers from training opportunities, is one example of this tendency. Such a policy obviously saves these employers money, but potentially increases calls on general taxation and upon individual employees, many of whom can ill afford to invest in skills. A better thought out and more explicit reconceptualisation of the balance of interests between state, employer, individuals (or their representatives) and society as a whole, would inform much of what follows.

One concrete expression of such a development would be moves by government and industry to shift towards a model of corporate governance that acknowledged the interests of groups other than simply shareholders, such as employees and the community. As the RSA's report on the future of the company makes clear (RSA, 1994), without such a broader definition of legitimate interests the ability to adopt a long-term perspective and achieve a better balance between the goals of the individual firm and of the communities within which it operates, will remain problematic. Kockan and Dyer (1992) go further, and argue that without a wider conceptualisation of the stakeholders in companies, the adoption of sophisticated systems of personnel management are unlikely within the Anglo-Saxon model of capitalism.

Industrial strategy – the missing context

At present VET policy assumes the creation of a high-skill economy, but this broad vision is not linked to any mechanism that might aid and monitor the development of a high-skills product strategy within any particular sector. There is simply a belief that such strategies will emerge across the entire economy as a result of market forces. As suggested above, this may not be the case.

How best are these concerns to be pursued? We would suggest through the creation of an integrative strategy for improving the competitiveness of the UK economy, a strategy centring on differentiation of goods and services from those of low-cost competitors through product innovation, high quality and high specification (Porter, 1990). The creation of a highly-skilled workforce would be one strand within this overall strategic approach.

It is certainly the case that, in most other developed countries, such as Germany, Japan, France, and the 'tiger economies' of the Pacific rim, VET policies are framed within the broader context of an industrial strategy. This strategy embraces a vision of the future development of the economy, which is expressed in terms broader than simple macro economic targets. The aim is to forecast which sectors and products will offer the best opportunities in future; to encourage investment in them and offer assistance to them through adjustments to the taxation system, infrastructure and skill supply mechanisms; and to tackle perceived weaknesses both in sectors of the economy and in the infrastructure that supports them. Issues of skill supply and demand are generally dealt with holistically within such strategies. Thus, Dr Shoichiro Toyoda, president of the Toyota Motor Corporation, suggested that, 'the purpose of national economic policy is to enable each citizen to manifest his potential fully in work to which he is well suited' (IMD/World Economic Forum, 1991).

In Britain this conceptualisation of economic policy is largely absent. Indeed, the idea of an industrial strategy has been anathema to the government (Chandler, 1994). However, a number of commentators on training policy (Green and Ashton, 1992; Senker, 1992; Chapman, 1993 and 1994) have argued that, in the absence of an industrial strategy, training policy makers and providers lack a contextual framework within which to direct their efforts.

With the abolition of NEDO and the NEDC, the institutional mechanisms that might design such a strategy are now lacking. Plainly, a prerequisite for an industrial strategy would be the creation of some new forum within which employers, government, and trade union representatives could be brought together to review economic progress and to plan for the future. Such a forum would act as the focus for long-term thinking about the development of appropriate plans for securing competitive strategies based upon higher skills and the provision of higher-quality goods and services. It would also need to address long-term structural problems within the economy, such as income distribution, and the system of industrial finance. Once such a forum and appropriate policies were established, it could help government (both central and local) bring to bear a variety of incentives, both negative and positive, which would help lead companies to adopt a longer-term perspective on competitive strategies.

Levers for change
Within the context of an industrial strategy, what types of incentives might be available to deal with skill supply and utilisation? The following are a selection of instruments that might be deployed, not as isolated initiatives, but as part of an integrated package of measures.

The tax system
Taxation has the potential to play an important role. The Institute of Personnel Management suggested, in its document *Towards a National Training and Development Strategy* (IPM, 1992) that a tax rebate, directed through employers' national insurance contributions, could be given to those employers 'who can demonstrate that they are making a serious investment in the skills of their employees (for example, by gaining the Investors in People award)' (IPM, 1992, p.9). One problem here may be the dwindling proportion of the workforce who are covered by NI. Increasingly, the weekly hours of part-time jobs means that employers pay no NI for these workers.

As an alternative to tax rebates, the imposition of some form of remissible training tax or levy has been regularly floated as a means to force employers to take training more seriously. A *Financial Times* survey of Training and Enterprise Council directors (Wood, 1993) showed a substantial minority (40 per cent) supported the imposition of a training levy, though a more recent survey by the CBI has shown lower levels of support among employers more generally (CBI, 1994b).

Legislation
Direct legislative intervention to impose rights and duties, with regard to both training and wider personnel issues, such as employee representation and involvement, may also be contemplated. In this regard it is worth noting that even today, the role of legislation (such as that relating to health and safety, the Food Safety Act, and industry-specific regulations like the Financial Services Act) plays a considerable role in placing a 'floor' under levels of training provision in Britain (Felstead and Green, 1994).

Indirect legislative action might also be considered. German notions of a qualifications requirement as a 'licence to practice' in various trades might be one method of tackling weaknesses in both product and service quality, and training. As Felstead and Green (1994, pp.212-213) point out, such requirements exist in Britain within a number of occupational labour markets which are administered by strong professional organisations, for example architects, accountants, and civil engineers. Calls for professional licensing to be extended to other occupational groups, for example estate agents, have been made in recent years, and might be encouraged, both by legislative intervention, and by pressure exerted by those with whom such groups have commercial dealings. Thus mortgage lenders and insurers could demand that all estate agents with whom they do business hold appropriate qualifications.

The supply chain
This brings us to the use of supply chain pressure. This was a concept which received enthusiastic support from NEDO, and which does appear within the auto industry to have had some effect upon the quality of production among motor component suppliers. Within retailing, Marks and Spencer are the leading proponents of such an approach. Worryingly, there is some evidence (Rubery, Tarling and Wilkinson, 1987) that other large British retailers have been exerting pressure on their suppliers to concentrate on low value added products.

Encouragement could be given to the wider use of positive pressure for higher quality via the supply chain, not least via public sector purchasing policies. Here, pressure could not only encompass contract compliance procedures covering training and quality minima, but also extend to the criteria governing the award of grants and aid from central and local government (including TECs). Thus, firms in the tourism industry would only be eligible to receive grants from the tourist boards if they met certain minimum standards of personnel and training practice.

Finally, the government could provide greater support for consumers and consumer groups. Enhanced consumer protection legislation and a climate of more active consumerism could help act as a lever for enhanced product and service quality.

Help and advice to business
The provision of support services, in terms of help and advice, that could enable small and medium-sized firms to adjust their product market strategies, redesign work organisation and job content, and implement more sophisticated forms of personnel management, would be extremely valuable. Despite all the energies that have been put into the development of DTI services to business, TECs, LECs, and 'one stop' advice centres, Britain still trails countries such as France and Germany in the amount and quality of advice and support that is available to business at a local, regional and national level (Bennett and McCoshan, 1993) In Germany the Länder, employer organisations, and the chambers of commerce; and in France employer bodies and the chambers of commerce (with significant support from the state), offer advice and consultancy services of a scale and quality that are frequently lacking here. Britain's problems to some extent reflect the weakness of its employer organisations and trade associations (Sisson, 1987). Without better resourced sectoral bodies, neither the development of product market enhancement strategies nor improvements in industry-specific training among small and medium-sized firms seems likely. Government arguably has a role to play in helping industry to tackle these structural weaknesses.

With an industrial strategy in place, and with a battery of measures available to incentivise a high skills competitive strategy, what types of labour market policies might complement these developments? It is to this question that we now turn.

A new labour market framework?
Government labour market policies establish a framework within which the employment policies of individual enterprises are set.

They also send powerful signals to employers about the directions in which labour market and employment conditions are expected to develop. In order for progress on skill utilisation and deployment to be made, what is required is a broad set of policies that can send coherent and consistent messages on a number of fronts. First, about the nature of the strategies that can provide sustainable, long-term competitive advantage, and, in particular, about the diminishing returns that are liable to attend attempts to proceed any further with competitive strategies centred on headcount reductions, casualisation, low wages, and de-skilling of significant sections of the workforce. Second, that in pursuing a competitive strategy based on higher levels of skill, the need is for not just more skills within the workforce, but also for personnel management systems, and methods of work organisation and job design that will provide an environment in which those skills can be deployed to maximum productive effect.

Within the context of attempts to reshape the labour market, a range of policies has been suggested that might contribute to pressure to improve skill utilisation. We begin by reviewing two currently fashionable policies that centre on adjustments to individuals' incomes as a means of improving demand and usage of skills.

A minimum wage. Minimum wages are almost back in fashion. Recent American evidence (for example, Card, 1992; Katz and Krueger, 1992) has reminded the economics profession of what it knew all along, but was often strangely reluctant to stress. This is that a minimum wage does not necessarily have harmful employment consequences. If workers are being paid the value of their marginal product, then a minimum wage that constrains employers to pay more than this will lead to them losing their jobs. However, if workers are being 'exploited' (that is being paid less than the value of their marginal product), then the imposition of a minimum wage will not have unfavourable employment consequences.

For some time now the adherents of wage regulation have gone beyond this and argued that regulation might be a lever for promoting economic efficiency. They argue that a minimum wage would force employers to enhance the productivity and skills of workers in order to make them affordable. This argument needs to be treated with care. At one level it is a version of an old argument that if a firm offers low wages to the majority of its workers and if this reflects their generally low productivity, then a minimum wage is not just a matter of sacking a few marginal workers. Rather, it will mean that the employer will not be able to afford to employ anyone. If the firm wishes to remain in business, it will have to get its act together and devise production strategies which make its workers sufficiently productive to be able to afford to pay them the legal minimum.

Though superficially attractive, this argument is little more than a statement of faith. Employers will often be unable to change their product strategies overnight. By way of analogy, if we were to try to increase the living standards of workers in a developing country by declaring (say) a doubling of their pay, the probable consequence would be mass unemployment. Those who believe that a minimum wage in Britain would have the very different effect that they suggest, would have to ague that the adoption of strategies to ensure higher productivity would be significantly easier than in a developing country. For some companies and sectors that indeed might be the case, but is far from obvious to us that it would generally be so. It may be that arguments for the introduction of a minimum wage based around issues of social equity make its imposition attractive (Commission on Social Justice, 1994). Its introduction might also have some force as a signal to employers that cost-based competition centred on low wage rates was to be discouraged. All we would argue is that the adoption of a minimum wage as a means to directly ratchet up demand for skills represents a significant gamble.

The social security system as a lever for economic efficiency
Some writers have argued that changes in the social security system might also provide a lever by which employers might be forced into a high skills strategy. The essence of this argument is that the workers could be enabled to be more selective about whether or not to accept a low-paying job. At the moment recipients of unemployment benefit or income support face a variety of availability for work tests whose harshness varies almost from year to year. The prevailing opinion is that such tests are necessary if 'scrounging' on the system is to be avoided. Similarly, those low paid in work who are in receipt of family credit are faced with a battery of rules which strongly discourage them from leaving work and relying instead entirely upon social security. In other words, the mainstream em-

phasis is upon minimising the work disincentives inherent in any scheme of income maintenance.

However, there is an alternative view which, to a degree, makes a virtue of such disincentive effects. For example, the adherents of Citizens Income suggest a system which would give every adult an unconditional cash payment each week or month. This is received regardless of other income, though obviously at some point the payment is in effect clawed back via income tax liabilities. One merit of Citizens Income, its supporters argue, is that excessively high marginal tax rates can be avoided as an individual's income rises. But this applies to those in work. If the unconditional payment were sufficiently large, it might discourage people from working at all. Advocates of CI make a virtue of this by arguing that the correctly calculated social benefits from not taking a dead-end, badly paid job and doing something else instead, are likely to be positive. This something else might range from pursuing a hobby, to taking care of the children, to charitable work, to full-time training or education. The arguments for and against this scheme are complex and beyond the scope of this paper, but one point is particularly relevant. This is that, by giving potentially low-paid workers more choice about what they do with their lives, CI would make it far more difficult for employers to successfully offer low-paid, low-skill jobs. However, the likely levels of CI that could be afforded in the foreseeable future suggest that any such leverage would be only marginal.

A securer labour market environment

If neither of the above options appear to offer suitable forms of leverage upon problems of weak demand for skill and poor skill utilisation, what other avenues are open to policy makers? We would suggest two that deserve further exploration.

The first concerns creating a securer labour market environment, in which risks and benefits are more equally shared between employer and employees, and where the development of flexible working patterns, which can bring benefits to both parties, are not confused with forms of casualisation. In this regard, efforts would appear to be necessary to discourage employers from utilising crude versions of the core/periphery dichotomy to legitimise the abandonment of any commitment (for example, to provide training) to large sections of their employees. In this respect, some form of training levy might have a role to play in encouraging employers not to neglect the provision of training opportunities for large sections of their employees (a third of the adult workforce according to Gallie and White, 1993)

More broadly, attempts need to be made to reconceptualise notions of flexible employment, to downplay the negative connotations that have attached to those of the workforce placed in the 'periphery' by their employers, and to strengthen the advantages that flexible working patterns can offer (Mouriki, 1994; Sidaway and Wareing, 1992). To take the example of part-time work, in other countries, such as France and Sweden, part-time employment is common across the whole occupational range, rather than as is so often the case in Britain, to low status, low-skill work (Mouriki, 1994; Sidaway and Wareing, 1992). Moreover, in Britain, but not in France and Sweden, part-timers generally experience significantly less advantageous terms and conditions of employment than do their full-time colleagues, and normally are much less likely to receive training. However, as Mouriki argues, this situation is not a fixed condition. A different approach to labour market regulation, and a programme of detailed reform could relatively easily transform the status and conditions of part-timers in Britain (Mouriki, 1994).

Personnel management systems for a skilled workforce
A second area that needs attention is the upgrading of personnel practices in many parts of the economy. As has been suggested above, there would seem to be a positive synergy between product market strategies that place a heavy emphasis upon quality and skill, and the use of sophisticated personnel practices of the developmental, 'soft' HRM type. If an industrial strategy could start to move competitive strategies away from over-reliance on low-cost competition, this would provide a more supportive environment for the encouragement of better personnel management. Such developments notwithstanding, it is important to acknowledge the scale of the obstacles that stand in the way of such an approach. British employers have tended to be content with piecemeal developments, to be hostile to any legislative framework of rights and duties (for example, on issues such as employee involvement and communication), and often to see advantage in the pursuit of greater degrees of casualisation. Reversing these trends will not be easy. As Sisson

points out (1994, p.42), for the widespread adoption of the 'soft' model of HRM to become a reality in Britain, 'there would have to be a fundamental reappraisal of the ways in which British companies are run', not just in terms of personnel strategies and systems, but also regarding the relationship between demands for short-term financial returns and long-term competitive success.

In pursuit of better personnel practice, such as formalised employee involvement, legislative and other forms of pressure, for example, the use of contract compliance, might be necessary. Moreover, external help, either through subsidised consultancy services, or better-supported employer and trade organisations, would probably be needed to enable many firms to contemplate redesigning work organisation and jobs in support of higher skilled competitive strategies. Finally, training initiatives would need to be targeted at those key groups most in need of change and help – managers, small businesses, and worst-performing sectors.

A new model of policy making on VET

The kinds of policy outlined above bring with them a requirement for new styles of policy formulation. To begin with, they demand much greater coordination between different parts of government. If the training problem is defined as being simply one component of wider structural difficulties with labour market operation and competitive and product market strategies within the UK economy, then it follows that the types of broad, integrative policy initiatives sketched above require the cooperation of a number of ministries and departments. To date, such cooperation has not been one of the strengths of the British system of government (Rosenhead, 1992; Ponting, 1986; Hoskyns, 1983 and 1984; Wilks, 1986).

If wider notions of stakeholdership are to take root in business, they must be reflected in the policy making. This means a less confrontational approach to policy formulation, the acceptance of notions of social partnership, and attempts to create and sustain genuine consensus about what will, of necessity, be controversial reforms (for a more detailed review of these issues, see Keep and Mayhew, forthcoming b).

It would also be valuable to inject a greater sense of realism into the debate about VET, so that participants (particularly employers) can put their cards on the table, and stop making motherhood statements about the need for more training which they often do not really believe. Employers have become adept at producing the correct responses to questions about the need for more and better training, particularly when the questions are being posed by or for a government department, such as the Employment Department. Thus, 90 per cent of employers questioned for an Employment Department-sponsored survey on employers' attitudes towards lifetime learning agreed that 'people should be encouraged to participate in education and training throughout their working lives' (Metcalf, Walling and Fogarty, 1994). The results of the survey showed however, that the same companies that provided this positive response were in many cases far from committed to giving any concrete effect to their beliefs. Frequently training was restricted to only some sections of the workforce, and the majority of employers were unwilling to provide any training that was not strictly related to the immediate job-needs of the worker – stances unconducive to fostering participation in lifelong education and training.

This gap between what employers say, and what they do, has caused significant problems for training policy. We need to move to a situation where Pavlovian responses to official enquiries cease, and where all the actors are willing and able to provide policy-makers with an honest view of current and likely future attitudes and intentions. Until this happens, VET policy is being constructed on sand.

Conclusion

A training policy paper which makes no mention of the reform of NVQs, TECs, or ITOs is unusual. Our thesis is that while the specific configuration of the institutional underpinnings of VET supply are undoubtedly important, they do not represent the optimal starting point for diagnosing or tackling Britain's problems in harnessing skills in the pursuit of increased international competitiveness. If more attention could be focused on the means of engineering a sustainable increase in the quantitative and qualitative demand for skills across the British economy lasting progress might be more possible. A policy thrust along these lines would have the effect of forming a more amenable backdrop to efforts to improve the mechanisms of skill supply, and pull from the demand side would also ease at least some of the problems that have dogged many recent training initiatives.

However, even if the argument which we have advanced is accepted, the implementation of the type of policy strategy we advocate remains problematic. Besides the likely resistance of many employers and of the City to the advancement of notions of stakeholder capitalism and the development of an industrial strategy, the realities of the political process and of political careers provide a formidable barrier to any shift away from treating the training problem as one that can best be tackled through schemes, initiatives, and special measures aimed at boosting skill supply. As the recent history of training policy attests (Ainley and Corney, 1990; Keep, 1986), the need to be seen to be doing something (and to be doing it swiftly) about perceived failures in training have tended to force governments and civil servants towards high-visibility 'quick fixes'. Moreover, as Rose (1991) notes, the dynamics of ministers' political careers produce incentives for policies that are based around swiftly-implemented initiatives that allow the individual to make his or her mark. The type of long-term, fundamental realignment of policies towards a wider conceptualisation of the 'training problem' and a focus on demand stimulation, would therefore require considerable political discipline on the part of any government. Not least because the full benefits of such a policy might not show through within the life of a single parliament. Short-termism is a feature of political as well economic life in Britain.

Despite these difficulties, and the complexities that would invariably confront anyone seeking to implement such a strategy, we believe that our case merits debate. At the start of this paper we pointed to the broad consensus that exists concerning the Reichian model of competitive advantage and the need therefore to move towards an economy where a highly-skilled workforce was the centrepiece of product market strategies based on supplying high quality goods and services. The reasons for this consensus are not hard to find. The underlying thesis of Reich's arguments appears sound, and the outlook in social and economic terms for any developed nation that cannot compete in terms of skill, looks bleak indeed, with increasing reliance on low-wage competition with the developing world (Commission on Social Justice, 1994). The need therefore, is to develop and implement policies that ensure that the economy makes a step change in its demand for and use of skills. The question is whether current policies can produce this change on a sufficient scale and with the necessary speed. If not, we are in for a bumpy ride.

References

Ainley P and M Corney (1990) *Training For the Future: the Rise and Fall of the Manpower Services Commission.* London: Cassell

Anderson T (1994) Unpublished PhD thesis. Denmark: Copenhagen Business School

Bennett R, H Glennerster and D Nevison (1992) *Learning Should Pay.* Poole: British Petroleum

Bennett R and A McCoshan (1993) *Enterprise and Human Resource Development.* London: Paul Chapman

Buxton T, D Mayers and A Murfin (1994) 'Research and Development and Trading Performance'. In *Britain's Economic Performance,* eds T Buxton, P Chapman and P Temple, pp.144-159. London: Routledge

Card D (1992) 'Do Minimum Wages Reduce Employment? A Case Study of California, 1987-89', *Industrial and Labor Relations Review,* vol.46, no.1, pp.38-54

Chandler G (1994) 'The Political Handicap'. In *Britain's Economic Performance,* eds T Buxton, P Chapman and P Temple, pp.9-30. London: Routledge

Chapman P (1993) 'The British Training Problem: Market Failure and Intervention'. Paper presented to the Centre for Economic Policy Research conference on The Skills Gap and Economic Activity. London: Birbeck College, 19/20 April

Chapman P (1994) 'Investment in Skills: Training Policy in the UK'. In *Britain's Economic Performance,* eds T Buxton, P Chapman and P Temple, pp.160-175. London: Routledge

Collinson D (1988) *Barriers to Fair Selection: A multi-sector study of recruitment practices.* London: HMSO

Commission on Social Justice (1993) *The Justice Gap.* London: Institute of Public Policy Research

Commission on Social Justice (1994) *Social Justice – Strategies for National Renewal.* London: Vintage

Confederation of British Industry (1987) *Investing for Britain's Future: Report of the City/Industry Task Force.* London: CBI

Confederation of British Industry (1994a) *Thinking Ahead: Ensuring the Expansion of Higher Education into the 21st Century.* London: CBI

Confederation of British Industry (1994b) *Flexible Labour Markets – Who pays for training?* London: CBI

Coopers and Lybrand Associates (1985) *A Challenge to Complacency: Changing Attitudes to Training.* Sheffield: Manpower Services Commission/National Economic Development Office

Cosh A, A Hughes, A Singh, K Carty and J Plender (1990) *Takeovers and Short-Termism.* Industrial Policy Paper No.3. London: Institute of Public Policy Research

Court G, H Connor and N Jagger (1994) *The IES Graduate Review 1994.* Sussex, Brighton: IES

Cutler T (1992) 'Vocational Training and British Economic Performance: A Further Instalment of the "British Labour Problem"?' *Work, Employment and Society,* vol.6, no.2, pp.161-83.

Delbridge R and P Turnbull (1992) 'Human Resource Maximization: The Management of Labour Under Just-In-Time Manufacturing Systems'. In *Reassessing Human Resource Management,* eds P Blyton and P Turnbull, pp.56-73. London: Sage

Department of Trade and Industry (1991) *Britain – the preferred location.* London: DTI

Dex S (1988) 'Gender and the Labour Market'. In *Employment in Britain,* ed D Gallie, pp.281-309. Oxford: Blackwell

Edwards P, M Hall, M Hyman, P Marginson, K Sisson, J Waddington and D Winchester (1992) 'Great Britain: Still Muddling Through?'. In *Industrial Relations in the New Europe,* ed A Ferner and R Hyman. Oxford: Blackwell

Employment Department (1985) *Education and Training for Young People,* Cmnd 9482. London: HMSO

Employment Department (1988) *Employment for the 1990s.* Cm 540. London: HMSO

Employment Department (1991) 'Into Work', *Skills and Enterprise Briefing,* Issue 15/91, October

Employment Department (1993) *Labour Market and Skills Trends, 1994/95.* Sheffield: ED

Employment Department (1994) *Labour Market and Skills Trends, 1995/96.* Sheffield: ED

Felstead A and F Green (1994) 'Training During the Recession', *Work, Employment and Society,* vol.8, no.2, pp.199-219

Finegold D (1992) 'The Implications of "Training in Britain" for the Analysis of Britain's Skill Problem: A comment on Paul Ryan's "How Much Do Employers Spend On Training?"', *Human Resource Management Journal,* vol.2, no.1, pp.110-15

Finegold D and D Soskice (1988) 'The Failure of Training in Britain: Analysis and Prescription', *Oxford Review of Economic Policy*, vol.4, no.3, pp.21-53

Gallie D and M White (1993) *Employee Commitment and the Skills Revolution*. London: Policy Studies Institute

Glynn S and H Gospel (1993) 'Britain's low skill equilibrium: a problem of demand?', *Industrial Relations Journal*, vol.24, no.2, pp.112-25

Goodman A and S Webb (1994) *For Richer, For Poorer: The Changing Distribution of Income in the UK, 1961-91*. London: Institute of Fiscal Studies

Goold M and A Campbell (1986) *Strategies and Styles: The Role of the Centre in Managing Diversified Corporations*. Oxford: Blackwell

Green F and D Ashton (1992) 'Skill Shortage and Skill Deficiency: A Critique', *Work, Employment and Society*, vol.6, no.2, pp.287-301

Hakim C (1990) 'Core and Periphery in Employers' Workplace Strategies: Evidence from the 1987 ELUS Survey', *Work, Employment and Society*, vol.4, no.2, pp.157-88

Harijan L (1991) 'New Technology, Management Strategies and Shop Floor Workers', PhD thesis (unpublished), University of Leicester

Hoskyns J (1983) 'Whitehall and Westminster: An Outsider's View', *Parliamentary Affairs*, vol.36, pp.137-47

Hoskyns J (1984) 'Conservatism is Not Enough', *Political Quarterly*, vol.55, pp.3-16

Hutton W (1995) *The State We're In*. London: Jonathan Cape

Hyman, J (1992) *Training at Work: a Critical Analysis of Policy and Practice*. London: Routledge

IFF Research Ltd (1994) *Skill Needs in Britain 1994*. London: IFF

Industrial Relations Research Unit (1994) 'Employment Relations 2000: Proceedings of a conference to launch the Centre for International Employment Relations Research', Warwick Papers in IR, No 50, July. Coventry: Warwick University, IRRU

Institute of Management (1994) 'Survey of Long Term Employment Strategies'. London: Institute of Management/Manpower (mimeo)

Institute of Personnel Management (1992) *Towards a National Training and Development Strategy*. London: IPM

International Institute of Management Development and the World Economic Forum (1991) *World Competitiveness Report*. Switzerland, Lausanne: IMD

Katrak H (1982) 'Labour skills, R&D, and capital requirements in the international trade and investment of the UK; 1968-78', National Institute of Economic and Social Research Discussion Paper No.51. London: NIESR

Katz L and A Krueger (1992) 'The Effects of a Minimum Wage in the Fast Food Industry', *Industrial and Labor Relations Review,* vol.46, no.1, pp.6-21

Keep E (1986) 'Designing the Stable Door: A Study of How the Youth Training Scheme was Planned', Warwick Papers in Industrial Relations, No.8. Coventry: Industrial Relations Research Unit

Keep E (1994) 'Vocational Education and Training for the Young'. In *Personnel Management,* second edition, ed K Sisson, pp.299-333. Oxford: Blackwell

Keep E and K Mayhew (forthcoming a.) 'UK Training Policy – Assumptions and Reality'. In *The Skills Gap and Economic Activity,* eds A Booth and D Snower. Cambridge: Cambridge University Press

Keep E and K Mayhew (forthcoming b) *The British Vocational Education and Training System – A Critical Analysis.*

Kockan T A and T Dyer (1992) 'Managing Transformational Change: The Role of Human Resource professionals', Proceedings of the Sydney conference of the International Industrial Relations Association. Geneva: IIRA

Lam A and D Marsden (1992) 'Shortages of qualified labour in Britain: a problem of training or of skill utilisation?', Paper presented to CEDEFOP conference on vocational training. Berlin

Lloyd C and M Rawlinson (1992) 'New Technology and Human Resource Management'. In *Reassessing Human Resource Management,* eds P Blyton and P Turnbull, pp.185-199. London: Sage

Marginson,P, P Armstrong, P Edwards, J Purcell and N Hubbard (1993) 'The Control of Industrial Relations in Large Companies: An Initial Analysis of the Second Company Level Industrial Relations Survey'. Warwick Papers in Industrial Relations No.45. Coventry: Warwick University, Industrial Relations Research Unit

Marsh P (1990) *Short-termism on trial.* London: Institutional Fund Managers' Association

Metcalf H (1988) 'Careers and training in tourism and leisure', *Employment Gazette,* pp.84-93, February

Metcalf H, A Walling and M P Fogarty (1994) 'Individual Commitment to Learning – Employers' Attitudes', ED Research Series, No.40. London: ED

Millward N (1994) *The New Industrial Relations.* London: Policy Studies Institute

Millward N, M Stevens, D Smart and W R Hawes (1992) *Workplace Industrial Relations in Transition.* Aldershot: Dartmouth

Mouriki A (1994) 'Flexible Working: Towards Further Degradation of Work, or Escaping from Stereotypes?', Warwick Papers in Industrial Relations No.49. Coventry: University of Warwick, Industrial Relations Research Unit

National Commission on Education (1993) *Learning to Succeed.* London: Heinemann

Neale A (1992) 'Are British workers pricing themselves out of jobs? Unit labour costs and competitiveness', *Work Employment and Society*, vol.6, no.2, pp.271-85

New C C and A Myers (1986) *Managing Manufacturing Operations in the UK 1975-1985*. London: British Institute of Management

O'Mahony M (1992) 'Productivity Levels in British and German Manufacturing Industry', *National Institute Economic Review*, no.139, February, pp.46-63

Oulton N (1993) 'Workforce Skills and Export Comptetitiveness: An Anglo-German Comparison', National Institutue of Economic and Social Research Discussion Paper No.47. London: NIESR

Organisation for Economic Co-operation and Development (1994) *Employment Outlook 1994*. Paris: OECD

O'Reilly J (1993) 'Functional Flexibility, Training and Skill in Britain and France', Surrey, Egham, Royal Holloway College, Centre for Management Studies, paper presented at the Department of Employment, May

Perry P J C (1976) *The Evolution of British Manpower Policy*. London: British Association of Commercial and Industrial Education

Ponting C (1986) *Whitehall, Tragedy and Farce*. London: Hamilton

Porter M (1990) *The Competitive Advantage of Nations*.

Prais S J (1989) 'How Europe would see the new British initiative for standardising vocational qualifications', *National Institute Economic Review*, 129, pp.52-4

Prais S J (ed) (1990) *Productivity, Education and Training*. London: NIESR

Prais S J (1991) 'Vocational Qualifications in Britain and Europe: theory and practice', *National Insitute Economic Review*, May

Pratten C (1990) 'The Limits to Training', *Financial Times*, 3 April

Price L (1994) 'Poor Personnel Practices in the Hotel and Catering Industry: Does It Matter', *Human Resource Management Journal*, vol.4, no.4, pp.44-62

Purcell J (1989) 'The impact of corporate strategy on human resource management'. In *New Perspectives on Human Resource Management*, ed J Storey, pp.67-91. London: Routledge

Rajan A (1993) *Where the New Jobs Will Be*. London: Centre for Research in Employment and Technology in Europe

Reeder D (1981) 'A Recurring Debate: Education and Industry'. In *Education and the State: Volume 1, Schooling and the National Interest*, eds R Dale, G Esland and M MacDonald. Lewes: Falmer

Reich R (1983) *The Next American Frontier*. Middlesex: Penguin

Rogers P and M Tran (1988) 'US feathers ruffled at British invasion', *The Guardian*, 26 April

Rose R (1991) 'Too Much Shuffling of the Cabinet Pack?', *Institute of Economic Affairs Inquiry,* No.27, September

Rosenhead J (1992) 'Into the Swamp: The Analysis of Social Issues', *Journal of the Operational Research Society,* vol.43, no.4, pp.293-305

Royal Society of Arts (1994) *RSA Inquiry – Tomorrow's Company: The Role of Business in a Changing World – Interim Report.* London: RSA

Rubery J, R Tarling and F Wilkinson (1987) 'Flexibility, Marketing and the Organisation of Production', *Labour and Society,* January

Senker P J (1992) *Industrial Training in a Cold Climate.* Aldershot: Avebury

Sewell G and B Wilkinson (1992) 'Empowerment or Emasculation? Shopfloor Surveillance in a Total Quality Organization'. In *Reassessing Human Resource Management,* eds P Blyton and P Turnbull, pp.97-115. London: Sage

Shackleton J R (1992) *Training Too Much?* London: Institute of Economic Affairs

Sidaway J and A Wareing (1992) 'Part-timers with potential', *Employment Gazette,* pp.19-26. January

Sisson K (1987) *The Management of Collective Bargaining – An International Comparison.* Oxford: Blackwell

Sisson K (1994) 'Personnel Management: Paradigms, Practice and Prospects'. In *Personnel Management,* Second edition, ed K Sisson, pp.1-50. Oxford: Blackwell

Smithers A (1993) *All Our Futures: Britain's Education Revolution.* Manchester University: Centre for Education and Employment Research

Soskice D (1993) 'Social Skills from Mass Higher Education: Rethinking the Company-based Initial Training Paradigm', *Oxford Review of Economic Policy,* vol.9, no.3, pp.101-113

Steedman H, G Mason and K Wagner (1991) 'Intermediate Skills in the Workplace: Deployment, Standards and Supply in Britain, France and Germany', *National Institute Economic Review,* no.136, May, pp.60-76

Temple P (1994) 'Evaluation of UK Trading Performance'. In *Britain's Economic Performance,* eds T Buxton, P Chapman and P Temple, pp.76-97. London: Routledge

Verma A and D Irvine (1992) *Investing in People.* Willowdale, Ontario, Canada: Information Technology Association of Canada

Walker D A (1985) 'Capital Markets and Industry', *Bank of England Quarterly Bulletin,* December, pp.570-575

Whipp R (1992) 'Human Resource Management, Competition and Strategy: Some Productive Tensions'. In *Reassessing Human Resource Management,* eds P Blyton and P Turnbull, pp.35-55. London: Sage

Wilkinson A, T Redman and E Snape (1993) *Quality and the Manager*. Bristol: Institute of Management

Wilks S (1986) 'Has the State Abandoned British Industry?', *Parliamentary Affairs,* vol.39, pp.31-46

Wood L (1993)'TEC chiefs call for wider action', *Financial Times,* 10 May

Worswick G D N (ed) (1985) *Education and Economic Performance*. London: Gower